Rx for Business

A Troubleshooting Guide for Building a High Performance Organization

Rx for Business

A Troubleshooting Guide for Building a High Performance Organization

Mark Graham Brown

Darcy E. Hitchcock

Marsha L. Willard

Chicago • London • Singapore

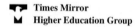

Times Mirror
Higher Education Group

Library of Congress Cataloging-in-Publication Data

Brown, Mark Graham.
    Rx for business : a troubleshooting guide for building a high
-performance organization / Mark Graham Brown, Darcy E. Hitchcock,
Marsha L. Willard.
      p.   cm.
    Includes index.
    ISBN 0–7863–0477–4
    1. Labor productivity. 2. Problem solving. 3. Employee
motivation. 4. Organizational learning. I. Hitchcock, Darcy E.
II. Willard, Marsha L. III. Title.
HD57.B765 1996
658.3' 14—dc20   96–3990

Printed in the United States of America
1 2 3 4 5 6 7 8 9 0 ML 3 2 1 0 9 8 7 6

Introduction

If you are a parent, you may have referred to home health care books when your children weren't feeling well. These books help parents diagnose the problem and decide what to do. In most cases, when parents use these manuals, they are not necessarily trying to cure the condition, but rather to validate what they are already planning to do (e.g., give the child an aspirin and call the doctor in the morning). The parents also want to know if there is something else they should know about. Is the rash unimportant, or could it be a symptom of something far more serious that requires immediate medical attention?

This book serves as a home health care book for managers who are trying to diagnose what's not working well in their organization. You'll be able to find answers to these and many more questions:

- **Strategy and Leadership:** Will your strategy ensure your competitiveness? Why aren't the employees buying into the corporate strategy? What must managers and executives do to "walk the talk"?

- **Implementation:** Why are your improvement efforts stalling? What should you do if you're trying to make a change in one small part of an organization and the rest of the organization is hoping you'll fail? What should you do when you have many improvement efforts competing for attention?

- **Structure and Systems:** How can you overcome fiefdoms so you can get something done? Which organizational structure is best for you? Are you measuring what is important or just what is easy to measure? Are you rewarding and reinforcing the behaviors you want?

- **People:** Are employees not performing well because (1) they don't know how to do the job, (2) they are poorly matched to the job, or (3) the job is poorly designed so no one can do it well? Why are employees bored and unhappy? How can you get people across the organization to share their learning?

- **Outside Influences:** What do you do when your suppliers are the biggest bottleneck you face in serving your customers? Are regulations preventing you from doing what's best for your stakeholders? Is your parent company underfunding your efforts?

To be fair, this book will not answer all of your questions, anymore than a home health book can cover every possible illness. If your stock is declining or your local area network just went down, you probably won't find a solution in this book. We have focused primarily on people problems—organizational performance problems that are affected by human interaction. In this information age where teamwork and organizational learning are increasingly important, these people problems can represent serious barriers to maintaining your competitiveness. Are you having trouble meeting customer needs or competing in the global market place? Are employees disgruntled? Is management confused about where the organization is going and why? If you have problems similar to these, this book should help you figure out why and what to do about it.

Through a series of questions and diagnostics, we'll help you pinpoint your organization's illness and then prescribe a course of action. We use symbols to help you understand what the action requires. We'll note which actions are particularly costly or difficult to do. We'll also indicate which treatments often require the oversight of a specialist. Here is a definition of the symbols you'll see throughout this book:

Expensive, often requires significant financial investment.

Takes lots of time.

Requires expert advice.

 Quick fix; may not be a long-term solution.

 Hard to do.

 Quick, easy, relatively painless, and usually a complete solution to the problem.

How to Use This Book

This book is not intended to be read from beginning to end. Instead, this book is more like a medical textbook or an automobile manual. When you first get the book, it might be helpful to leaf through it to familiarize yourself with the content. Then, when you are troubled by something at work, take a guess as to where the problem might lie. Then turn to the appropriate chapter to learn more about the symptoms, causes, and possible actions. IF YOU DON'T FIND AN ANSWER, BE SURE TO TURN BACK TO THE EARLIER DIAGNOSTICS TO TRY ANOTHER PATH. Sometimes it takes more than one try to find a practical solution to your problem. You can also use the index to reference a specific problem by its symptom.

Through a series of diagnostics, we'll help you narrow down the root cause of your organizational illness and then select a treatment. Figure 1 shows how to navigate through this book.

Figure 1: Four Steps to a Solution

Step 1: Select a chapter.
Review the Preliminary Diagnosis chart in this Introduction and select a chapter that seems to address the problem you are facing.

Preliminary Diagnosis

Part I: Strategy and Leadership

Vision/strategy. Leaders haven't set priorities and direction that will ensure the organization's long-term success. (See Chapter 1)

Communications. Leaders have set direction, but employees are not aware of it or don't understand it. (See Chapter 2)

Requirements. Leaders have not identified the key success factors needed to achieve the long-term vision. (See Chapter 3)

Behavior. Leaders understand what is necessary, but have not yet aligned their behavior. (See Chapter 4)

Part II: Implementation Issues

Approach. We do not have a coherent, systematic approach to performance improvement. (See Chapter 5)

Scope. Our change effort is not working because it is not being implemented uniformly across the organization. (See Chapter 6)

Pace. We are trying to change too much too quickly, or we are getting started too late and doing too little. (See Chapter 7)

Part III: Structure and Systems

Measures. Our measures don't give us a complete picture of the health of our organization. (See Chapter 8)

Structure. Our structure makes it hard to get things done. (See Chapter 9)

Feedback. We don't always know how well we are doing. (See Chapter 10)

Reinforcement. We reinforce and reward the wrong things. (See Chapter 11)

Part IV: People

Personality and core abilities. We don't seem to have the right people to get the job done. (See Chapter 12)

Motivation. What employees want and the organization needs are incompatible. (See Chapter 13)

Knowledge and skills. People don't know how to do it right. (See Chapter 14)

Shared learning. We are missing opportunities because we don't know how to leverage or act on our shared learning. (See Chapter 15)

Part V: Outside Influences

Regulations. Regulations inhibit us from doing the right things. (See Chapter 16)

Involuntary alliances. Critical stakeholders will not allow us to do what we need to be successful. (See Chapter 17)

Voluntary alliances. Our "partners" are inhibiting our progress. (See Chapter 18)

Global trends. The future does not bode well for us because of what's happening in the world. (See Chapter 19)

xi

> **Feedback.** We don't always know how well we are doing. (See Chapter 10)

Step 2: Identify a possible cause.
Each chapter begins with a brief discussion of the possible problems as well as a chart of symptoms and causes. Review the symptoms and select a likely cause. If none of the symptoms sound like the problem you're having, go back to step 1.

---

10 Feedback

We don't always know how well we are doing.

Feedback is the cornerstone of continuous improvement. Stepping on the scale regularly is what keeps us to our diets. Similarly, without current, relevant data about how well it is doing in its key business indicators, an organization will be ill-equipped to maintain a competitive edge. Getting the right information to the right people, however, isn't always as easy as it seems. Review the list of symptoms below to see if any match the difficulties your own organization may be having with closing the feedback loop.

Symptoms	Causes
People don't know how well they are doing. (1, 2)	1. Employees don't get enough timely, relevant feedback.
The right information doesn't seem to get to the right people. (1)	2. Employees don't know how to interpret the data.
People don't understand the feedback they get. (2, 3)	3. Employees don't know how to act on the data.
By the time we get the information, it's old news. (1)	4. The people who give the feedback don't understand the job.
People ignore the feedback they get. (2, 3)	5. The feedback contributes to conflict and finger pointing.
We are uncomfortable giving feedback. (4, 5)	

119

> 3. Employees don't know how to act on the data.

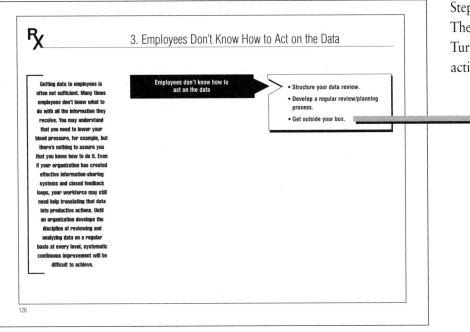

Step 3: Read about the cause and identify an appropriate action.

The remainder of the chapter is a discussion of the causes and their treatments. Turn to the likely cause and review the possible actions. If none of the causes or actions seem appropriate, go back to step 2 to select another path.

R X 3. Employees Don't Know How to Act on the Data

Getting data to employees is often not sufficient. Many times employees don't know what to do with all the information they receive. You may understand that you need to lower your blood pressure, for example, but there's nothing to assure you that you know how to do it. Even if your organization has created effective information-sharing systems and closed feedback loops, your workforce may still need help translating that data into productive actions. Until an organization develops the discipline of reviewing and analyzing data on a regular basis at every level, systematic continuous improvement will be difficult to achieve.

Employees don't know how to act on the data

- Structure your data review.
- Develop a regular review/planning process.
- Get outside your box.

• **Get outside your box.**

126

Step 4: Learn more about the action.

On the facing page is an explanation of each possible action. Where appropriate, we have also provided additional references so you can learn even more. The complete citation for every reference is provided in the bibliography at the end of this book. If none of the actions solve the problem you're having, go back to step 3 to select another possible cause.

Structure Your Data Review

Many employees, especially those new to data analysis, are unsure of how to process feedback. Share this simple four-step process for examining and acting on feedback:

1. Review and assess. Examine the feedback and explore your reactions to it. Is it satisfactory feedback? Does it reveal problems? How closely does it meet your goals? If there are problems, which are of highest priority? This last question helps the work group focus its energies.

2. Determine root causes. Whether the feedback is good or bad, you should understand the causes. If the feedback is good, you will want to know what you need to do more of in order to maintain or improve the results. If the feedback is negative, you will need to know where to perform problem solving for the highest leverage.

3. Action plan. After completing the first two steps, you will need to determine your next steps. If the causes of the data cannot be explained, you will need to design an experiment to learn more about your processes. If the data revealed problems, you will need to design and implement solutions to improve results. If the feedback was good, you will want to identify what you can do to achieve the next level of excellence.

4. Check effectiveness. Check that your actions have had the desired results. Adjust your plan as needed and reenter the process again at Step 1.

For more information on team problem-solving and design of experiments, see *An Introduction to Team-Approach Problem Solving* by Jones and McBride and Montgomery's *Design and Analysis of Experiments*.

Develop a Regular Review/Planning Process

The structured process described above is not meant for use only when there is a problem or aberration in feedback data. Organizations need to be disciplined in their use of feedback and make the examination of data a regularly occurring event. The process described above provides a useful outline for business planning meetings. Basing business planning on feedback data assures the relevancy of planning decisions and discourages decision making based on hunches. Conduct an annual business-planning meeting that uses past performance data to establish new goals. Then follow the format described in the preceding section to structure quarterly meetings (or more frequently if needed) to review progress and design corrective or improvement actions. For a complete description of one method, see Chapter 9 in Hitchcock and Willard's *Why Teams Can Fail and What to Do about It*.

Get Outside Your Box

Many times work groups are hampered by their myopic view of things. They can look at information and not see the possibilities for innovative action. When we are accustomed to doing a job a certain way, it becomes very hard to conceive of truly creative innovations. Consider some of these strategies for generating creative solution options to your team's problems.

• Conduct brainstorming sessions. Adhere strictly to brainstorming rules (go for volume, no evaluation, build on earlier ideas, be "off the wall"). Sometimes it's helpful to set minimums (no discussion until we have at least 30 ideas).

127

Get Outside Your Box

Many times work groups are hampered by thei of things. They can look at information and no bilities for innovative action. When we are a doing a job a certain way, it becomes very hard truly creative innovations. Consider some of thes generating creative solution options to your tea

How to Get Started

Your first step is to try to narrow down your problem. If you had a medical problem, you might ask, Where does it hurt: your head, stomach, or foot? In this case, you need to determine where your organization hurts. Is the problem at the head of your organization with leadership and strategy, or do you have the right strategy but the implementation is flawed? Are you having trouble with the anatomy of your organization, that is, its systems and structure? Do your troubles seem to stem from the employees themselves or does your organizational illness stem from something outside your organization? These questions are addressed in different parts of the book.

Review the statements in the following Preliminary Diagnosis section and see if any sound like the problem you're having. The statements are cross-referenced to chapters. Once you find a statement that seems to describe your situation, turn to the indicated chapter to more clearly define what ails you.

Chances are you don't have just one problem; and some of your challenges may be interrelated. To help you take a "systems approach" to improving your organization, we have provided a worksheet at the end of the text. Use it to help you see patterns and relationships. Look for recurring causes and recommended solutions so you can solve several problems at once.

Preliminary Diagnosis

Part I: Strategy and Leadership

Vision/strategy. Leaders haven't set priorities and direction that will ensure the organization's long-term success. (See Chapter 1)

Communications. Leaders have set direction, but employees are not aware of it or don't understand it. (See Chapter 2)

Requirements. Leaders have not identified the key success factors needed to achieve the long-term vision. (See Chapter 3)

Behavior. Leaders understand what is necessary, but have not yet aligned their behavior. (See Chapter 4)

Part II: Implementation Issues

Approach. We do not have a coherent, systematic approach to performance improvement. (See Chapter 5)

Scope. Our change effort is not working because it is not being implemented uniformly across the organization. (See Chapter 6)

Pace. We are trying to change too much too quickly, or we are getting started too late and doing too little. (See Chapter 7)

Part III: Structure and Systems

Measures. Our measures don't give us a complete picture of the health of our organization. (See Chapter 8)

Structure. Our structure makes it hard to get things done. (See Chapter 9)

Feedback. We don't always know how well we are doing. (See Chapter 10)

Reinforcement. We reinforce and reward the wrong things. (See Chapter 11)

Part IV: People

Personality and core abilities. We don't seem to have the right people to get the job done. (See Chapter 12)

Motivation. What employees want and the organization needs are incompatible. (See Chapter 13)

Knowledge and skills. People don't know how to do it right. (See Chapter 14)

Shared learning. We are missing opportunities because we don't know how to leverage or act on our shared learning. (See Chapter 15)

Part V: Outside Influences

Regulations. Regulations inhibit us from doing the right things. (See Chapter 16)

Involuntary alliances. Critical stakeholders will not allow us to do what we need to be successful. (See Chapter 17)

Voluntary alliances. Our "partners" are inhibiting our progress. (See Chapter 18)

Global trends. The future does not bode well for us because of what's happening in the world. (See Chapter 19)

Acknowledgments

Writing this book—a troubleshooting guide to effective performance improvement strategies—has required that we exploit the knowledge of many great thinkers and practitioners of our time. We are infinitely grateful to the authors of all our listed references, for their writings have enriched us.

In addition, we want to thank by name those individuals who took the time to give us specific advice and assistance:

Tanis Cordes, The Private Industry Council

Dave Kenney, ADC Kentrox

Diana Larson and Sharon Buckmaster, SOTA Consulting

Alan Lindsay, Pacific Learning Systems

Tamsen Wassell, New Work Dimensions

Ron Wigger, OMI

Thanks also go to our editor, Cindy Zigmund, for being a great advocate, and to Terri Knicker for her assistance in polishing sections of the text.

Contents

PART I

STRATEGY AND LEADERSHIP

The key to a successful business strategy is to do something well that others seem to falter at or cannot do well at all. Deciding on your own strategy means capitalizing on your strengths and finding a market niche that may not currently be served by others. Once you have identified a success strategy, the leaders in the organization need to create the vision, the plan, and the systems to take the organization where it needs to go. Strategy is not to be set in stone; it is to be reviewed and readjusted as business and economic conditions change. If you suspect that your organization suffers from a problem with your strategy or leadership, review the statements below and select the chapter that appears to address your most troubling problem.

Vision/Strategy	Leaders haven't set priorities or direction that will ensure the organization's long-term success.	Chapter 1
Communication	Leaders have set direction, but employees are not aware of it or do not understand it.	Chapter 2
Requirements	Leaders have not identified the key success factors needed to achieve the long-term vision.	Chapter 3
Behavior	Leaders understand what is necessary, but their behavior is inconsistent with the vision and long-term goals.	Chapter 4

1 Vision/Strategy

Leaders haven't set priorities or direction that will ensure the organization's long-term success.

Sometimes people die prematurely because they fail to change habits and behavior patterns that were established early in life. We are so consumed with the struggles of day-to-day life that we don't take the time to plan for our future or make the necessary lifestyle changes to ensure a bright future. Since organizations are a collection of people, they tend to have the same problems. Companies are so busy addressing the day-to-day operational issues of running their businesses and meeting current stakeholder's needs that they don't spend enough time thinking about where they want to be in the future or planning how they will get there. If you don't have a direction and a plan, chances are that you are going to end up somewhere you may not want to be. . . and it may be too late to turn back or change course. In this chapter we will examine why some companies lack a vision for the future, and we'll suggest actions that you can take to help ensure that you have a practical, worthwhile vision for your organization's future. To begin your search, review the symptoms list on the next page and identify the most likely cause of your difficulties.

Symptoms

Employees feel that there is no clear direction for the company. (1)

Employees do not agree with the vision or believe that it can be accomplished. (2)

Employees cannot explain their role in helping to achieve the vision, nor can they translate the vision into action. (3)

The same strategy has been in place for years. Customers change, the business climate changes, but the strategy remains the same. (4)

We're having trouble competing. (4, 5)

Causes

1. Vision/strategy are vague.

2. Vision is unrealistic and probably unachievable.

3. Vision/strategy are not communicated properly.

4. Vision/strategy are not adequate to ensure long-term success.

5. Executives don't know what the vision should be.

Now turn to the cause that seems to be the most likely source of your problem.

1. Vision/Strategy Are Vague

Experience indicates that many organizations spend little time planning the future direction for their company. Some simply focus on day-to-day survival as their goal, while others have a vision of being the biggest and best company in their field. Since the advent of the quality movement, it has become quite fashionable to write vision statements. Often a great deal of time and effort is put into these vision statements, but when employees respond with boredom and blank stares to the new vision statement, executives remain perplexed. Clarity is important in a vision. A vision statement should tell employees where the organization is going and be clear enough to let them know when they have achieved the goal. If your vision is vague or unclear to employees, here are some actions that may sharpen its focus.

Vision/strategy are vague

- Rewrite or rethink the current vision statement.
- Develop vision statements for individual units, locations, or areas.
- Develop measurable goals to clarify the vision.

Rewrite or Rethink Your Current Vision Statement

A good way to test the clarity of your vision statement is to pick half a dozen employees at random and ask them to write a paragraph explaining what the company vision statement means. If you get widely different answers, the vision is probably unclear. The first thing you need to do is make sure that you eliminate jargon. Words and phrases such as *world-class*, *benchmark*, *market-driven*, *customer-focused*, and *value added* are often meaningless to employees. A common phrase seen in many mission statements is "Be a leading supplier of . . . ." Does this phrase mean the biggest, the best, or just good enough to participate in a market area? Phrases such as leading supplier are not good choices for vision statements because they are unclear. Another approach to making your vision clear is to develop it into a slogan or catchy phrase that people will remember.

A company in the corn milling business wanted to double its business in five years and struggled with the words needed for its vision statement. The vision statement it ended up with was: Two million by 2000. The company was hoping to double its production level from 1,000,000 bushels of corn per year to 2,000,000 per year by the year 2000. Employees loved this vision statement because it was clear and easy to remember. The beauty of this vision statement is that it is not only simple but also specific enough so that the company will know if it achieves this vision.

Some general guidelines for writing vision statements include:
1. The vision should not be more than one or two sentences in length (a single sentence is best).
2. The vision should be specific enough so that it could not be applied to another company.
3. The vision should describe where you want to be in your industry or marketplace and when you plan to get there.

Develop Vision Statements for Individual Units, Locations, or Areas

Another way to improve the clarity of an organization's vision is to require individual business units or locations to develop their own specific vision statements that outline how they will help the company achieve its overall vision. The problem employees often have with the company's vision is that it is too far removed from what they do in their jobs or locations. Be aware that you must be careful when developing "cascading" vision statements for each part of the business. The statements may end up looking much like the overall vision and do nothing to add clarity or give individuals a sense of their role in helping to achieve the vision. A vague mission statement for the whole company leads to vague vision statements being written by its business units or locations. In developing a specific vision statement for a business unit or location, it is important to define exactly what the subordinate organization will need to do to help the parent company achieve its vision. When defining a vision statement for a subordinate organization, you need to

• Make sure the vision is *linked* to the overall vision of the organization. Employees need to see that by achieving their unit's vision, they are contributing to the overall effort of the company.

- Make sure the vision is *specific*. It has to be easy for employees to understand.
- Make sure the vision is *realistic* and *meaningful*. Employees must believe that they can achieve it.

A vision statement developed for the sales and marketing department of the corn milling business might be Increase sales by 15 to 20 percent per year over the next five years. This statement tells employees what they need to achieve and the time frame for accomplishment. Employees in the sales organization need to know that in order to double production in five years, product sales must also double. By increasing the sales goals each year, the company is able to support increased production and achieve its overall vision. Once the vision statement is decided upon, it is up to each unit in the organization to translate the vision into specific action plans.

Develop Measurable Goals to Clarify the Vision

Sometimes it is okay to have a vision statement that is somewhat vague, as long as you clarify it with measurable goals. For example, let's suppose that an organization has a vision that states: Become the highly recognized market leader in providing on-line information to the home. This statement is quite vague because of the phrase "highly recognized" and the lack of a defined target market. However, we could make this vision statement much clearer by enhancing it with listing the following long-term, measurable goals:
- Increase the number of on-line subscribers in our current market area (Puget Sound) by 1,000,000 by January 1, 1998.

- Add additional West Coast markets, targeting Portland area by 1997 and northern California by 1998.
- Expand the on-line services to capture greater market share.
- Have our company name mentioned in at least 40 regional publications per year and 25 national publications per year.
- Achieve revenues of $100 million next year.

Now, the vague vision statement about being highly recognized is sharp and clear. All of the goals listed are measurable and relate to the overall vision of being a market leader in providing on-line information to the home. The key to making a vision statement work is to set goals that are directly related to the vision, make them measurable, and base the goals on research. In other words, don't make up the goals. Do enough research on your target markets, your competition, and the economic conditions to make certain that your goals are realistic for your organization. Once your goals are defined, create specific action plans to achieve each goal. For further information on establishing measurement systems, see *Vital Signs* by Steve Hronec.

A vague vision of where you want to be is much easier to fix than an unrealistic vision. Organizations tend to want to be the biggest and the best in the market and commonly don't spend a lot of time thinking about the plausibility of their grandiose visions. The fallacy of this thinking is that we set our sights on an unrealistic target and are happy if we can get even half-way there. Is bigger really always better? Being number one in any market always makes you the target for competition at every angle. Some organizations have found that smaller is better and that they can be quite successful without being the major supplier in the markets they serve. If you suspect your vision is unrealistic and probably unachievable, consider some of the actions outlined in this section.

Vision is unrealistic and probably unachievable

- Conduct research on market and competitive factors.

- Focus the vision on one or two key performance measures.

- Be happy without being the biggest or the best.

- Adjust your vision as your situation changes.

Conduct Research on Market and Competitive Factors

Unrealistic vision statements often result from a lack of research to identify what might be possible in the marketplace. When executives develop a vision for the organization's future, they all too often do so without any prior research on the market opportunities and on the competitive and economic forces in the market. They may develop vision statements in a completely arbitrary fashion. For example, a major financial services firm decided that its vision was to double in revenue size in three years. This growth would certainly be a stretch, but when the executives were challenged about the plausibility of this vision, they could not provide data or evidence to support the feasibility of the vision they had just created nor were they cognizant of the resources they would need to accomplish their vision. Doubling revenue in three years is a major accomplishment that requires the company to make a certain level of resource commitment. In addition, the executives failed to consider the overall changes that continue to occur in their marketplace. A great many more competitors were now in their market because the number of companies that offer financial services had increased significantly.

To create a realistic vision statement, you need to know what is happening in your market. A cellular phone manufacturer wanted to double its production and revenue in one year. Given that cellular phone service is a high-growth market, this vision is realistic for the company because it knows that its products will be in demand. The company's biggest problem is making the phones fast enough without sacrificing quality.

It's also very important to know what your major competitors are up to. You can bet that your competitors have visions that involve growth and increased market share. Some competitors might be directly focusing their attention on stealing customers from you. In fact, one credit-card company wrote the following vision statement: Put American Express out of business.

American Express ought to know that this competitor is aggressively going after its business before developing its own vision statement. When you are the major market player, you will inevitably become the target of smaller companies who will devise strategies to erode your market position. Finding out as much as you can about the strategies of your competitors will help you develop a vision statement that is realistic and attainable.

Focus the Vision on One or Two Key Performance Measures

Vision statements are problematic when they are too broad or all encompassing. It is often not practical to try to be all things to all people and it is unrealistic to think that it is possible. Not every company can be the biggest or the best in the marketplace. In fact, trying to be the biggest is often a mistake. Larger organizations often have many problems that smaller companies don't have. Although remaining small may be the key to ensuring an organization's future success, you rarely see an organization whose vision is to remain small and maintain a 5 percent market share. Rather than trying to be the biggest and best, concentrate your vision on one or two performance factors. For example, one organization had a vision stating that it wanted to maintain current revenue levels but earn $3,000,000 in profit before taxes. The beauty of this vision is that it focused everyone's efforts on activities that would reduce costs and bring in high-margin sales. Trying to do too many things at once will dilute your effort and make improvement activities disjointed.

Be Happy without Being the Biggest or the Best

Isn't it funny that you never run across a company who has a vision to be number three or number four in its market? Why is it that everyone wants to be number one? There are thousands of companies and organizations in the world that will never be number one, or the best at what they do, but they are still quite successful. It is better to establish a vision that is realistic and attainable, even if it involves being less than the biggest or most successful. More vision statements should include statements such as Move from number 15 to number 10 in the markets we serve. It is good to have high aspirations, but developing a vision statement that is totally unrealistic will fail to enlist the support of your employees whose help you need to achieve your vision.

Adjust Your Vision as Your Situation Changes

Once the vision statement is approved and plastered all over the walls of the company, executives are frequently reluctant to change it, even when it becomes obsolete. When a significant amount of time and money is spent getting each word just right and communicating the vision to employees, management may not scrap the vision and formulate a new one when necessary. Attaining 30 percent market share in Pacific Rim countries may have seemed reasonable three years ago, but if this year you realize that it will not be possible because one of your competitors has beaten you to the market with products that were better and less expensive than yours, you need to change your vision. A vision statement should be reviewed every year, at the very least, to evaluate whether or not it is still reasonable. Once you've engraved the vision on bronze plaques and posted them all over the company facilities, it becomes more difficult to change. Therefore, it makes sense to keep the vision on paper so it can be revised in response to changing market situations.

We worked with a manufacturing company whose vision is to be the "last ice man." In other words, the company manufactures a product whose market is expected to disappear or at least be substantially smaller over the next 10 years. Being the last ice man is not exactly a motivating vision for employees who may wish to retire from the company some day. A vision should be realistic, but it should also inspire employees and help motivate them toward achieving the vision for the company's future. If you believe that your vision is too shortsighted, or not adequate enough to ensure future success, here are some actions to consider to increase your chances for success.

Vision/strategy are not adequate to ensure long-term success

- Consider alternative products/services.

- Consider new markets for existing products/services.

- Focus on future growth opportunities.

Consider Alternative Products/Services

The company whose vision is to be the last ice man has actually taken some steps to ensure its future success by purchasing another company that makes similar products for which there is a better and longer-lasting market. This particular company was known for the one specific product that it invented. By limiting its vision to this product, it was doomed to becoming smaller and smaller as the demand for the product continued to shrink. Once it broadened its vision and realized that it could branch out into the manufacturing of other related products, the future became much brighter. In analyzing its own manufacturing facilities, the company realized that it would be prohibitively expensive to convert its equipment to produce the new products. Consequently, the best course of action was to purchase another company that already had the necessary equipment in place. Although the acquired company had a fairly small market share, the new owner was able to use its marketing and customer service expertise to grow market share for this new acquisition.

When considering new products or services, it is important to stay close to what you already do. Your business has probably established a reputation as being good at providing certain products or services. Therefore, it may be hard for potential customers to see you as anything else. Ford makes great cars, but it might have trouble manufacturing washing machines. While it could undoubtedly do a good job, since a washing machine is much less complex than a car, the public might not feel comfortable buying a Ford washing machine. Even if you can convince potential customers that you can diversify, you might not actually be able to make the transition well. A number of companies have gotten into trouble trying to get into businesses that they didn't know much about.

If you need to expand your business into other products or services to ensure your future success, consider the following suggestions:

- Explore how existing products or services can be modified.

- Concentrate on products or services that can be sold to existing customers who already know and trust you.

- Invest in adequate marketing programs to communicate your new capabilities to potential and existing customers.

- Think hard about your own capabilities and weaknesses before offering a new product or service.

Consider New Markets for Existing Products/Services

Another (and easier) way to ensure your future success is to sell your existing products or services to new customers. You may be able to identify potential customers that you have not even considered. For example, perhaps government organizations are even a market for your service though you have always sold to industry.

For years A&W sold its root beer only through its own root beer stands. Its draft root beer is still one of the best summer drinks available, but finding an A&W root beer stand is pretty tough these days. The company knew it had a unique product, so it devised an alternative marketing strategy by selling root beer in bottles and cans through the grocery stores.

Many critics thought that retail sales would hurt sales of the draft root beer in A&W restaurants. Just the opposite occurred, however. Root beer sales from restaurants maintained at existing levels with small growth, but overall sales dramatically increased.

If you can expand and grow your business by using alternative marketing strategies or by pitching your products/services to new customers, you have a quick and easy way of ensuring your future success.

Some companies limit their vision by focusing on local customers or by focusing on one particular method of selling their products. For example, a number of retail stores have been very successful selling through mail order catalogs. The Pottery Barn, a chain of home furnishings and accessories stores, began publishing mail order catalogs several years ago, and its sales have increased dramatically. Victoria's Secret started out as a mail-order catalog business. Since being purchased by The Limited, it has opened retail stores in just about every mall in the country and sells almost as much lingerie from the stores as it does from the catalogs.

Focus on Future Growth Opportunities

Companies are often guilty of neglecting future growth opportunities because they are concentrating on achieving short-term profits. They cut back on research, training of employees, marketing, and other areas to make the bottom line look better this quarter. By doing so, they are often mortgaging their futures. A number of companies with healthy profits right up until the end have gone out of business. The key to ensuring you don't trade off short-term financial results for future growth is in the amount of attention senior management gives to these factors.

The Lithium Division of FMC Corporation made its focus on future growth very visible by including developing a new source of lithium ore as one of its four major performance measures. A chemical company we worked with also became more future focused by measuring growth on the percent of sales from new products each year. Measuring growth and investing in the development of new products and services is not enough by itself. If measurement alone improved performance, no one with a bathroom scale would be overweight. More important than the act of measurement is the attention given to the data. Companies often measure new product development and growth, but these statistics rarely get as much attention as more short-term financial indexes. It's often said that what gets measured gets done. In our experience, what gets attention from senior management is what gets done.

2 Communication

Leaders have set direction, but employees are not aware of it or don't understand it.

Have you ever gone to the doctor and come away not really knowing your condition? The doctor explains your condition in complex medical terms; you nod your head, listen intently, and try to catch all that is being said, but when you walk out of the office, you realize that you did not fully understand what the doctor told you. When someone asks you to summarize the medical report you probably cannot do a very good job. If the doctor had used layman's terms, chances are that you would have come away with a better understanding. If the doctor had taken more time with you, shown graphs and charts of what was happening, and compared your condition to something you were familiar with, chances are that you would have understood even more.

One of the keys to good communication is to convey the message in terms that the audience can understand. A message on health awareness delivered to a group of grade school children will be very different than one delivered to a group of cardiac care patients over the age of 50. Communications must be tailored to the audience.

In addition, communication must happen continuously. If you returned to the doctor to continue your conversation, you would probably know quite a bit more after the second visit. Communication increases awareness.

Communicating the vision and strategy so that all employees understand the direction is vitally important in an organization. Employees can't help you reach your goal if they have no idea where the organization is going. If you feel that your organization's vision and strategy have not been communicated properly to the employees, examine the symptoms and focus on the corrective actions that this chapter presents in order to boost the communication efforts in your organization.

Symptoms

Employees are not aware that the company has a stated vision or direction. (1)

Employees commonly complain that management never tells them anything and they feel as though they are left in the dark. (2)

Employees cannot explain their role in helping to achieve the vision. (3)

There seems to be a "disconnect" in your communication because the intended audience is not receiving the message. (2, 3)

Causes

1. Direction and vision are only partially communicated because sensitive information is included.

2. Communication methods or media fail to get the message to employees.

3. Employees cannot relate their own efforts to the vision or future direction of the company.

Now turn to the cause that seems to be the most likely source of your problem.

1. Direction and Vision Are Only Partially Communicated Because Sensitive Information Is Included

In order to get everyone working toward achieving the vision, employees at all levels need to understand it. The leaders of the organization may purposely withhold information about the company's future from employees because they are afraid that the information might be leaked to competitors. Every company has some strategic information that is very sensitive and should be communicated on a need-to-know basis rather than globally throughout the organization. This is acceptable, as long as employees feel that they have *enough* information to work with and are not being left in the dark. Therefore, organizations must work hard to ensure that employees feel informed and receive regular updates from management. Not all employees will understand that management will not communicate sensitive information, but this secrecy is just a fact of life in today's competitive environment. Companies live and die by executing strategies. Management makes decisions each day that may not make sense to employees, but managers may be working with many more facts than the average employee is aware of. What is crucial is that an established relationship of trust exists between employees and management so that employees feel that they generally know where the company is headed and the plan to get there. The details can be saved for management meetings.

Direction and vision are only partially communicated because sensitive information is included

- Develop an abbreviated version of the vision statement that can be safely communicated.

- Communicate the vision and strategies for specific units or facilities in the organization.

Develop an Abbreviated Version of the Vision Statement that Can Be Safely Communicated

Sometimes the company's future direction or vision actually does contain sensitive information that should not be leaked to the media or to competitors. For example, let's say that your organization wants to double in size over the next five years and one of your key strategies is to acquire competitive companies in important markets. Without knowing elements of the strategy, employees may have no idea how you expect to achieve the vision. Worse yet, if your organization happens to be in a stable or shrinking market, employees may see the vision as completely unrealistic. If you really can't share parts of your strategy with employees, you should create a sanitized version of your vision and strategy that *can* be shared. Employees need to know what you want them to help you attain.

For example, a vision statement might focus on growth in a certain market or product line without revealing company plans to purchase a competitor company.

Communicate the Vision and Strategies for Specific Units or Facilities in the Organization

Another strategy for dealing with a vision or strategy that must be kept partially secret is to develop specific strategies and goals for various business units or divisions of the company. Employees in the business units do not need to know the overall corporate vision or strategy as long as they know where their business unit is going and how it will get there. We recommend that you develop business-unit–level vision statements and strategies even if you can share the corporate vision and strategies with employees. Relating the vision to the work being done in specific organizations helps everyone see his or her contribution more clearly.

Many companies do a very poor job of communicating the vision, values, improvement strategies, and other information linked to the strategic direction of the organization. A typical approach is to post this information on plaques that are prominently displayed in strategic spots around the facilities. Having done that, many companies feel that employees should surely "get the message." Some expand on the plaques and posters by printing the vision and values on the back of everyone's business cards or by handing out laminated wallet cards that are imprinted with the vision, values, and key business drivers to all employees. Once employees are able to carry around the company slogans, they should surely understand and internalize them. When interviewed, 9 out of 10 employees can't name the company vision, values, and key success factors. They don't pay much attention to the cards and certainly don't internalize the vision and values.

Communication must suit the targeted audience, and it must be repeated often, and in different ways, to be truly effective. The old adage, Tell them what you are going to say, tell them, and then tell them what you just said, works well because it ensures that your message is conveyed to the audience. Repetition is effective! The following pages provide recommendations for improving your communication with employees about the future direction of the organization.

Communication methods or media fail to get the message to employees

- Adapt communication methods to suit the characteristics of the audience.

- Measure the effectiveness of the communication.

- Use multiple methods and media to communicate the direction and vision for the organization's future.

Adapt Communication Methods to Suit the Characteristics of the Audience

The basic rule of communication is to know your audience. If you do not know your audience, you cannot tailor your message or your delivery style to fit its needs. For example, if more than half of your employees speak Spanish as their primary language, you would obviously want to communicate the vision and values in Spanish as well as English. Another thing to consider is the average reading level of your audience. Even many college graduates read at the 10th grade level, so writers must tailor their language to fit the audience. If you choose to communicate in writing, make certain that you use the appropriate reading level. Better yet, if employees are poor readers, consider communicating using an audiovisual medium. A slide presentation or multimedia presentation may capture people's attention more completely than a traditional speech by one of the company's executives.

To make sure that the future direction of the company is clearly communicated, we recommend that you make use of many different media and that you communicate your message frequently. It is important to vary the communication methods and frequency. Once employees become familiar with a message or medium, they will stop listening to the message. For example, if the vision and values are always printed on the second page of the monthly newsletter, after the first few newsletters, employees will no longer pay any attention to it.

Measure the Effectiveness of the Communication

One reason that organizations continue to use ineffective methods to communicate vision and strategy information to employees is that they don't realize that the methods don't work. In other words, they don't take the time to measure whether or not the message has gotten across to employees. You can use several very simple methods to measure the effectiveness of your communication. One way is to give a brief quiz to a randomly selected sample of employees. The quiz should ask questions about the organization's vision, values, key success factors, goals, and so on. Another approach is to select employees at random while walking through an office or plant area and ask them about the future direction of the company. A more formal approach to measuring the effectiveness of the communication might be a survey that is given to all or a large sample of employees. Keep in mind that you are evaluating understanding. You don't care if employees can recite the words in the vision statement or list the values word for word. You want to be certain that they understand the essence of where the organization wants to go in the future. The feedback you get from using any of these approaches will help you determine the effectiveness of your communication.

Use Multiple Methods and Media to Communicate the Direction and Vision for the Organization's Future

If you're not sure of the best way to communicate with your employees and don't have the time to measure how well your communication methods work, the safest thing to do is use many different methods and media to communicate the company's direction and strategy to employees. Typical methods used in organizations include the following:

• Displaying the vision and values on every employee's computer so that people can see them whenever they sign-on.

• Reviewing the vision and values at the beginning of every training class.

• Printing the vision and values in a different location in every issue of the company newsletter.

• Giving each employee a paperweight, or similar useful item, which includes the vision and values.

• Holding meetings periodically for all employees to review company progress toward achieving the vision. Town hall meetings work well because managers can give employees time to ask questions and discuss current business issues.

• Producing a video that explains the future direction of the company and the means or plans for getting there. This video can then be used at a variety of internal company meetings to get the message out to employee groups.

A combination of any of these methods will increase awareness across the organization. To increase the cost effectiveness of communication, conduct an informal survey of your audience to find out what types of communication they respond to and deliver your messages accordingly. When you use a variety of communication methods, employees are more likely to hear your message.

3. Employees Cannot Relate Their Own Efforts to the Vision or Future Direction of the Company

Employees may understand where the company wants to go in the future (vision) and how it intends to get there (strategy), but they cannot determine how their own jobs relate to this vision. The link between what the employee is doing and what the company wants to accomplish is missing. For example, an aerospace company's vision was to increase the value of the company as measured by stock price and other variables. In fact, the company made the vision very explicit by stating that it wanted the stock price to rise to $55 per share by the year 2000. Employees understood this, but most had no idea what they could do to influence the price of a share of company stock. Management had to spell out specific links between factors (such as the quality of workmanship and the cost to manufacture and the financial performance and market performance of the company) in order to educate employees on how they contributed to raising share price and thereby increasing shareholder value. In this section, we'll discuss actions that you can take to communicate the link between the vision and individual jobs in your company.

Employees cannot relate their own efforts to the vision or future direction of the company

- Link individual employee goals or objectives to key aspects of the vision/strategy.

- Develop a matrix linking functional areas to responsibility for achieving components of the vision.

Link Individual Employee Goals or Objectives to Key Aspects of the Vision/Strategy

Pacific Bell has done an excellent job in linking every employee's work to the company vision. The vision is somewhat vague and paints the picture of being a world-class telecommunication and information services company. To give the vision statement focus, each major business unit in Pacific Bell has developed a few key priorities on which to concentrate its improvement efforts. For example, Shared Services is a large group of support departments such as real estate, logistics, and safety/environmental. Shared Services has focused on four priorities:

• Increasing internal and external customer satisfaction levels.

• Reducing costs.

• Improving key work processes.

• Increasing employee job fulfillment.

All performance goals for the vice president in charge of Shared Services are tied to these four priorities. The same is true for all employees in the organization, including the employees in the mail room. By linking all employees' individual performance objectives to these four priorities, the vision becomes very real. It also becomes very clear to each employee how his or her performance relates to achieving the vision. Once all employees are working toward common goals, they can accomplish great things. Over the last several years, Shared Services has managed to reduce its operating costs by over 50 percent, while receiving scores of 95 percent satisfaction from internal and external customers!

Roadway Express of Akron, Ohio, is another example of a company that does well at linking individual employee responsibilities to its vision. Central to the vision is that all employees have to achieve a balance of satisfying what Roadway calls the "three voices":

• The voice of the customers.

• The voice of the employees.

• The voice of the shareholders.

All employees' performance goals are linked to specific achievements in each of the three areas.

The only way to have a true measure of how well you are achieving the company's vision and strategies is to link division, unit, and individual performance goals to that vision. By rolling up the achievements, your company can gauge progress toward the goals.

Develop a Matrix Linking Functional Areas to Responsibility for Achieving Components of the Vision

The link between individual job responsibilities and the company's strategies for achieving its vision can be established through the use of a matrix. Building a matrix that indicates the responsible area or individual, the level of responsibility, and the performance goals helps to make a very clear connection between individual and functional unit performance and the overall performance of the company. When this approach is used, it becomes clear to employees that everyone cannot do things that will impact all of the strategies or goals. To build a matrix, list the major goal areas and strategies along the left side of the chart and the functional areas in the company horizontally along the top. Develop a coding system to indicate responsibility level (e.g., 1—primary responsibility; 2—secondary responsibility; 3—supporting responsibility; and 4—no influence). Code each cross section so that everyone in the organization understands his or her role in executing strategies and achieving the vision. Those designated with primary responsibility for aspects of performance are considered responsible for execution, measurement, and results reporting. For example, if part of the company's vision is to increase sales by 30 percent, primary responsibility might lie with marketing/sales, which needs to increase sales prospects and closures, and with R&D, which needs to enhance existing products and develop new products for the salespeople to sell.

Organizations that have used this approach usually produce posters of the matrix and display them throughout the company.

More detailed versions of the matrix should be prepared for individual functions in the company. These matrices should specify the assigned responsibilities, the strategies and tactics to be executed, the individual(s) responsible for execution, and a target date for completion. Progress toward the vision and goals can then be monitored throughout the organization.

3 Requirements

Leaders have not identified the key success factors needed to achieve the long-term vision.

The obvious goal in all patient care is to return the patient to full health. As we know, that is often easier said than done. Successful patient care is based on a plan for care, especially in chronic or life-threatening illnesses. In planning for any care, the doctor must look at the symptoms, identify the underlying causes, and then determine the best treatment alternatives. Alternatives are weighed based on their side effects and potential for positively impacting the patient. To examine alternatives, doctors consult other medical professionals, read the most current research reports, and use their own experiences to prescribe the treatment that they believe will be most successful for their patients. All in all, doctors must determine the key requirements for patient care based on their patients' needs.

If they do not plan patient care and simply treat one symptom after another with no thought to their relationship or to the causal effect of one treatment to another, they are not considering the whole aspect of patient care and are unlikely to be very successful in solving the root problem. Often teams of doctors provide patient care for those with serious or life-threatening illness; together they can concentrate on the key care objectives and provide more comprehensive, coordinated patient care.

Organizations, like doctors, need to identify those factors critical for success. If you simply identify the goal, but have no idea what factors require focus to get you there, it is unlikely that you will wind up where you want to be. Short- and long-term strategies need to be devised and executed, and progress measured, to ensure the organization is on track to goal. Critical to this process is identifying key performance factors that can move the company forward. In this chapter we will

24

examine the reasons why key success factors are not properly identified and present actions that you can take to help ensure that your organization is focusing on the right performance indicators.

Symptoms	Causes
Measures used by the organization don't tell whether it is making progress toward achieving the vision. (1)	1. Emphasis is placed on the wrong performance factors.
The vision seems beyond what the organization can accomplish with current resources. (2)	2. Company lacks the capabilities or resources needed to achieve the vision.
The organization lacks focus for achieving the vision. (3)	3. The key success factors are too generic or lack focus.
No apparent plan is in place to achieve the vision. (3)	

Now turn to the cause that seems to be the most likely source of your problem.

1. Emphasis Is Placed on the Wrong Performance Factors

In order to differentiate your organization from the competition, you need to identify the customer's critical needs (e.g., low cost, fastest delivery, highest quality) and be the best performer in the marketplace in meeting those needs. A number of organizations fail to achieve their goals because they focus on the wrong strategies or performance factors. For example, they improve their service levels while maintaining high prices and then watch competitors steal market share by concentrating on being the lowest cost provider. Then they cut costs to improve profits and watch as customers leave because of poor service or inferior product. Determining what position you want to occupy in the marketplace and the strategies to be used to achieve or maintain that position requires a great deal of work and thought. Doing what's easy or logical is often not the path to success. We'll examine actions to improve your strategy to make certain that you do achieve your long-term vision for success.

Emphasis is placed on the wrong performance factors

- Conduct research to determine how performance improvements will lead to better results.
- Establish and communicate priorities.
- Conduct an experiment in a segment of the business.

Conduct Research to Determine How Performance Improvements Will Lead to Better Results

There is a story about a company that underwent an amazing transformation. It implemented a Total Quality Management (TQM) effort and managed to dramatically improve the quality of its products. When it began TQM, the defect rate was approximately 500 to 600 per million products. The company managed to reduce the defect rate to less than 50 defects per million products. It also improved the percentage of on-time deliveries from about 85 percent to 98 percent! This achievement took more than five years to accomplish and was a massive effort for the organization. In fact, the company even got ISO 9000 certified in the process and was a finalist for its state-level quality award, which is based on the Malcolm Baldrige National Quality Award criteria.

What do you imagine happened to performance factors such as sales, market share, and earnings? Was there a dramatic increase? Quite the contrary, none of the factors improved. Major improvements in quality and on-time delivery did not result in increased business from customers. It turned out that customers were happy with the company's past level of quality, and although delivery performance was not great, they could live with it. What drove customers' buying behavior was price. In order to pay for all the improvements in quality, the company had to raise prices slightly, and customers just weren't willing to pay for the improved quality. The lesson in this story is that you need to do research before you embark on an improvement effort to find out if the improvement will really lead to increased market performance for your organization. If customers are unwilling to pay for the improvements in quality or other aspects of performance, or if they just don't care, you may be investing much time and effort in a worthless strategy.

Finding out the key variables that influence customer buying behavior requires detailed market analysis and research. Your analysis should indicate trends in buying behavior when performance factors such as price, quality, and delivery service are adjusted. In addition, conducting primary market research such as surveys or focus groups will tell you what customers say or believe is important. The trick is to check the accuracy of what research reveals against actual buying behavior. In some cases, what customers tell you is important may not be what actually impacts their behavior. For example, airline customers list comfortable seats as their most important requirement when selecting an airline. However, customer behavior indicates that two other variables really control their selection: price and flight schedule. Make certain that you do enough research on performance factors to isolate those that are important to your customers and then work toward improving those factors so that the investment will be beneficial to your business.

Establish and Communicate Priorities

Sometimes the vision is clear, but it is so all-encompassing and challenging that employees are not sure where to concentrate their efforts. Let's say your vision is to be the biggest, best, most profitable, and most admired company for your environmental and community involvement efforts. This vision may be just too much to tackle. It is certainly all right to have a vision that includes many dimensions, but in those cases you may have to pick an aspect or two to concentrate on in the short term. For example, many working people have a vision of retiring comfortably by the time they reach age 60. Achieving that vision requires careful planning, investing, and levels of income and spending that will allow the worker to save enough money to reach that goal. It might be better for the worker to focus his or her efforts on one or two areas of the vision. For example, a statement that might add clarity to the retirement vision is: Invest a minimum of $10,000 per year in long-term, growth-oriented investments that yield an average return of 10 percent per year.

Organizations that do the best job of getting employees at all levels to work toward achieving the vision usually focus on a limited number of priorities. For example, the Lithium Division of FMC Corporation of Chicago has a broad vision statement that covers many dimensions of performance. However, one of its key measures and areas of focus is to develop a new site for mining lithium. By concentrating its efforts, the organization is able to focus its resources to achieve the goal. Once that goal is achieved, the key area of focus for the organization will shift to accomplish another dimension of the vision.

Conduct an Experiment in a Segment of the Business

One way to ensure that you focus your efforts on the right dimensions of performance is to actually conduct an experiment or pilot test in a segment of the organization. By selecting a representative sample or segment of the business, you can change performance factors and evaluate the impact that change has on your business before implementing the change across the entire company. For example, let's say that you have decided that the key to improving sales in your fast-food restaurant chain is to offer a number of small, low-cost items selling for less than $1.00. To pilot this new program, you need to select one region or a group of restaurants in which to test this new pricing/menu strategy. Implement the strategy and, after a sufficient length of time, measure and compare sales in restaurants with and without the new pricing/menu in order to evaluate the success of this new approach.

Companies that sell commodity-type products, such as agricultural goods, chemicals, or other raw materials, often use service as their differentiating factor. Since prices are often determined by the market place, service and supply are among a limited number of performance factors that they can control. Experiments or pilots are conducted in the same fashion in these types of businesses. A small segment of the business, such as a few product lines or a division, should be selected, and programs should be instituted to improve service. Factors such as market share, sales, and repeat business that would be expected to improve as a result of better service need to be monitored, evaluated, and compared with results in similar areas of the business where service is not improved. Only by conducting experiments like these will you be able to gauge the true likelihood of success of your performance improvement efforts. Otherwise, it may be very frustrating and costly to engage all employees in an effort to improve some aspect of performance and later find out that customers don't really care about it.

2. Company Lacks the Capabilities or Resources Needed to Achieve the Vision

One of the most common mistakes organizations make is failing to understand the limits of their resources. In this age of cost control with increased performance, the tendency is always to push the machinery or people up to or past their capability. Pushing the limits is often rewarded by increased performance in the short run, but there are long-term costs. Equipment tends to break down more frequently and require more service when it runs continually at capacity, and employees end up getting ill or having the pressure to perform impact their personal lives, which in turn impacts job performance. It is difficult for individuals and organizations to admit that they have limits and that there are some things they cannot do, at least without guidance or additional resources. Understanding your own limits and bringing in extra help or resources when necessary is one of the foundations of success. It is too bad that this lesson is often learned only through a painful series of failures.

In this section, we will review actions that you can take once you realize that you may not have the capabilities or resources to achieve your goals.

Company lacks the capabilities or resources needed to achieve the vision

- Buy the capabilities needed for success.
- Establish joint ventures with other businesses.
- Develop internal capabilities.
- Rethink the vision—go back to Chapter 1.

Buy the Capabilities Needed for Success

One way to get capabilities that exceed the present capacity of the organization is to purchase them. Unfortunately, some companies that have attempted to become larger and more successful by buying slightly related businesses have failed. Sony's purchase of Columbia Pictures caused the company to lose millions in 1994. Like many companies, Sony executives may have believed that business skills are generic and transferable. The thought process is that if you're good at running one type of business, you will probably be good at running other types of businesses. Sony, and others before them, have found that this is not necessarily true. Acquisitions must be well thought out, and there should be enough synergies between the two companies to make the combination a good fit. Random acquisitions to achieve a vision of getting bigger will probably be less than successful. The focus should always be on building upon your core competencies. (For more information, see "The Core Competence of the Corporation" by C. K. Prahalad and Gary Hamel.) Make sure that you have the capabilities to achieve your vision; buy the capabilities needed if you don't possess them.

In many cases, "buying capability" simply means hiring or retaining employees who know the business and can help you achieve the results you're looking for. Some companies are reluctant to search outside the organization to hire for key positions. Those on the executive management team may have started as trainees and worked their way up the ladder while learning the business. Companies that cling to this type of culture sometimes fail because they are unwilling to realize that they do not have the expertise internally to achieve their vision. They select an internal candidate to head up a new business unit because he or she has been successful at running other company business units. This does not always work if the businesses and markets are very different. Hiring someone from the outside allows the company to acquire the perspective and expertise it is lacking.

Companies lacking resources may be prevented from achieving their vision. If you establish some grand vision for your future success, you need to make certain the company has or can get the resources it needs to accomplish the vision. For example, a small, local company might want to become a major player in national markets, selling to Fortune 500 companies. If it does not take into account the marketing, production, and distribution networks needed to become a national sales organization, it may not realize that the goal is way beyond its reach. An expansive vision usually has a correlating need for facilities, capital, and a plan for resource acquisition that rarely accompanies the vision.

Establish Joint Ventures with Other Businesses

An increasingly popular way to expand an organization's capabilities, promote growth, and add value is the joint venture. Some organizations have carried this approach to its extreme, forming joint ventures to produce specific products or services and dissolving them as quickly as market needs change. By combining forces with other companies that possess a key competency that you need, you may become a formidable force in the market. For example, one of the world's largest grain producers is involved in a joint venture with a vitamin company to produce vitamin E. The grain company is able to extract the raw material that the vitamin manufacturer uses to produce the vitamins. The vitamin company lacked the facilities to extract the raw material from the grain, and the grain company lacked the processing expertise to convert the raw material into vitamin E, bottle, and distribute the product. It turned out to be a good match because both partners contributed a key area of expertise to the joint venture. For more information on joint venturing, see *The Virtual Corporation* by William Davidow and Michael Malone or *When Giants Learn to Dance: Mastering the Challenge of Strategy, Management, and Careers in the 1990's* by Rosabeth Moss Kanter.

Develop Internal Capabilities

If there is no great urgency for you to develop new competencies to achieve your vision, rather than buying expertise, it may be better to develop it on your own or by partnering with another organization. Obviously, this approach takes longer than buying the capabilities or forming a joint venture, but it may be the best long-term solution because the company retains the expertise internally and remains self-reliant.

Developing expertise internally requires a thoughtful plan. It begins with identifying the specific knowledge, skills, and abilities needed for various levels of personnel as well as identifying the necessary technological and capacity-related resources. Companies often have difficulty determining what their people need, and typically, this area requires the least systematic approach. For more information on a systematic approach to developing employee knowledge and skills, refer to Chapter 14 or *The Training and Development Strategic Plan Workbook* by Raynold A. Svenson and Monica J. Rinderer.

Most successful organizations concentrate on identifying and developing their core competencies in a limited number of areas. In other words, they identify what is required for future success and focus on being very good at it. The approach is simple, but in the 1980s when we were busy restructuring, decluttering, and delayering, the thought of "sticking to our knitting" was not at the forefront. Domino's pizza is an example of a company that identified its core competency and exploited it. Domino's makes and delivers pizza faster than anyone in the business. What makes Domino's better than others? The pizza may not be the best tasting or the cheapest; however, it is delivered the fastest, is the most consistent, and the most fairly priced. Federal Express is another example of a company that focuses on doing one thing and doing it better than the competition. Federal Express almost always delivers your package to the correct destination on time.

Organizations are often reluctant to focus their attention on a limited number of performance factors because they fear that the factors chosen may not give them the edge they need in the marketplace. That is why it makes sense to spend a significant amount of time studying performance factors and market responses and then carefully selecting those upon which you will place your focus. If you find that your organization is not properly focused, the following actions may help you to bring more clarity and focus to your organization.

The key success factors are too generic or lack focus

- Limit success factors to four to six major performance variables.

- Identify performance measures to track performance on key success factors.

Limit Success Factors to Four to Six Major Performance Variables

When companies initially want to identify the key success factors that they need to focus on to achieve their vision, the typical output is a list of 15 to 20 factors that are quite generic. Key success factors often include

- Competitive pricing
- Highly skilled employees
- On-time delivery
- Defect-free products/services
- Motivated workforce
- Innovative new products/services

While all of these things are certainly important, they are probably important for just about any company. Key success factors need to be specific to your business and market segments. Key success factors should answer the question What do we have to do to differentiate our products/services from our major competitors? Often, the answer to this question is employing one or two competitive strategies. For example, Granite Rock, a small company that won a Baldrige Award, concentrates on two key success factors: (1) being the lowest cost supplier of cement and gravel and (2) getting customers in and out of the quarry faster than any of its competitors. The key to success is in selecting the factors that will actually give you an edge over the competition. Granite Rock decided not to focus on quality, because rocks are rocks. The quality of the product must meet certain standards in order to be sold, so product quality is relatively similar no matter where you buy your cement or gravel. Consequently, other factors influence customer buying decisions. Granite Rock found that price was its key performance factor because state and local government offices were its primary customers and, the lowest bid was almost always awarded the contract.

Identify Performance Measures to Track Performance on Key Success Factors

Sometimes an organization has successfully identified key success factors but has no way of tracking performance on each of these factors. For example, consider a company that identified competitive pricing as one of its key success factors, but its performance measurement system did not have a method to track anything related to pricing. A cellular phone service company identified flexible rate plans as a key success factor for its business but did not have a method to measure the results of rate-plan flexibility. Without measures that are tied to the success factors in place, a company cannot track its progress. For guidance on developing measures that link to key success factors, see "Putting the Balanced Scorecard to Work" by Robert Kaplan and David Norton. The Malcolm Baldrige National Quality Award criteria are also good sources of information on this topic. The Baldrige criteria specifically look for evidence that an organization has derived performance measures from its key success factors.

4 Behavior

Leaders understand what is necessary, but have not yet aligned their behavior.

It is quite easy to understand that you need to change your behavior; it is an entirely different thing to actually do it. Changing behavior takes continuous, conscious effort and usually turns out to be a lot of work. Take, for example, the cardiac patient who is recovering from a heart attack and emergency bypass surgery. The doctor will prescribe a new diet and exercise program for the patient and caution him to avoid the foods and lifestyle that contributed to his current problems. The patient knows that in order to survive, he must change his behavior. Now, if the patient has not exercised in the last 40 years and has eaten bacon and eggs for breakfast every morning of his life, he is likely to resist some of the recommended changes. Intellectually, he may want to do all the right things, but executing the behavior changes may be hard to do and therefore, in his mind, not worth doing. Education plays an important role in fostering behavior change. If the patient is not properly educated on how to make the modifications in lifestyle and diet, he may not know that some of his behaviors, such as smoking, are harmful to his health.

The leaders of an organization, just like the patient, may know exactly what they should be doing but may be distracted by other issues or may believe that it is too difficult to make the necessary changes. The leaders may have good intentions, but not realize that their behaviors are inconsistent with the vision. If you believe that the leaders of your organization do not behave in a manner consistent with the stated vision of the organization, examine the symptoms and focus on the corrective actions presented in this chapter to align their behavior(s) with the vision.

Symptoms

Leaders' behavior and actions are inconsistent with the vision. (1)

Leaders don't "walk the talk"; they pay only lip service to the vision. (1, 2)

Leaders don't cooperate because there is no incentive to do so. (3)

Some leaders have made it clear that they are not supportive of the vision. (3)

Causes

1. Leaders lack the knowledge or skills to align their behaviors with the vision.

2. Leaders do not receive adequate feedback on their behavior.

3. Lack of planned positive or negative consequences.

Now turn to the cause that seems to be the most likely source of your problem.

1. Leaders Lack the Knowledge or Skills to Align Their Behavior with the Vision

The quickest test to determine whether people really need training is to ask them to perform the desired task and observe their performance. If they are fully competent in the task, they will be able to perform well. If they can't do it, or take an inordinate amount of time to do it, they may lack the necessary knowledge or skills. In these cases, training is appropriate. Managers are no different than other employees in the organization. They may lack knowledge or skills that make accomplishing an assigned task difficult.

The worst thing we do is to assume that leaders know how to accomplish their tasks simply because of their level in the organization. This assumption may set up the leaders and the organization for failure. Training may be appropriate to show managers how to match their management style to achieving the organization's vision. If managers do not seem to be grasping a new management style or executing it well, they may need a bit of guidance on how to change their leadership practices to be consistent with the organization's vision and values.

The following actions may help you find ways to give your leaders the knowledge and skills they need to embrace a leadership style consistent with the vision.

Leaders lack the knowledge or skills to align their behavior with the vision

- Train executives to use leadership practices that are consistent with the vision and values.

- Require executives to teach leadership courses to their direct reports.

- Arrange for executives to attend a national conference that features presentations by executives in world-class organizations.

- Arrange for executive site visits to companies with cultures that resemble the one you are trying to create.

Train Executives to Use Leadership Practices That Are Consistent with the Vision and Values

 Often leaders really want to change the culture, but they don't know how to manage or act differently. They want to embrace a more democratic leadership style, empower employees, and encourage employees to make more decisions on their own, but those concepts and styles may be very different from the ones they successfully used to move up the corporate ladder. If there is evidence that your executives really do lack the skills to change their behavior, some leadership training is in order. Much of the packaged leadership training on the market today is not really designed to change behavior, but it is designed to be informative. Executives may learn about management theories and perhaps complete a management-style assessment survey. The courses are usually very interesting and fun; however, after a few days out of the classroom and back on the job, attendees forget the material and slip back into their old habits.

The key to making leadership training effective is practice. You can learn the basics of golf or tennis in a couple of lessons, but you will spend months, or sometimes years, mastering the skills needed to play either game even moderately well. The same can be said of leadership skills. One cannot expect a three-day workshop to produce a major change in executive behavior. The best leadership courses include extensive practice, through simulation exercises, and planned follow-up to ensure that the skills learned in the classroom can be applied on the job. For more information on changing leadership style, see *Bringing Out the Best in People* by Aubrey Daniels or *Reinventing Leadership: Strategies to Empower the Organization* by Warren Bennis and Robert Townsend.

Require Executives to Teach Leadership Courses to Their Direct Reports

 The best way to get people to learn is to require them to teach the material to others. Xerox, Moore Business Forms, and a number of other successful organizations have used this approach to implement their leadership and customer-satisfaction training programs. Executives attend leadership courses and special train-the-trainer sessions where they learn to teach the courses to others. Each member of the senior executive team then teaches one or two sessions to managers at the next lower level. These managers teach their direct reports, and so forth. This is an expensive way to implement leadership training, but it is effective. It not only ensures that managers master the knowledge and skills taught in the courses but also helps to hold each level of managers accountable for keeping their behavior consistent with the leadership techniques they taught. This strategy also sends a very strong message to employees: The new leadership style must be very important because the executive team is spending a significant amount of time on overseeing its proper implemention.

Arrange for Executives to Attend a National Conference That Features Presentations by Executives in World-Class Organizations

We all have a tendency to turn to our peers for advice because they are most likely wrestling with the same issues we are. Executives can learn a great deal from listening to or spending time with executives from other organizations. Listening to an executive from a respected organization talk about what he or she *personally* did to help make the organization world-class can be very enlightening. David Kearns, former CEO of Xerox; Bob Allen of AT&T; or Jamie Houghton, CEO of Corning, have inspired many other executives to look for and make the necessary changes in their behavior and in the organization.

If you belong to an industry organization (e.g., The Conference Board), encourage your executives to attend and participate in relevant workshops and meetings sponsored by the organization. Industry groups are generally able to attract senior executives from some of the best companies in the world to participate in their sessions. Another source for executive interaction is the annual conference held in Washington, D.C., where recent Baldrige Award winners discuss how they transformed their organizations. Your executives will hear from executives from some of the best run companies in America and have a chance to network with executives from many other organizations that are going through culture-change initiatives similar to your own.

Arrange for Executive Site Visits to Companies with Cultures That Resemble the One You Are Trying to Implement

Another option is to send executives on a site visit or benchmarking visit to an organization whose culture is where you would like yours to be in three to five years. The advantage to this approach, as compared to attending a conference, is that executives have the opportunity to speak at length with executives from a company whose culture you are trying to emulate. Executives at Air Products and Chemicals learned a great deal about what they had to do to change their behavior by spending time with executives at Baldrige-winner Eastman Chemicals. The visitors found that because the companies' businesses were quite similar, they encountered many of the same problems in their attempts to become more customer focused.

If you are going to take your executives on a site or benchmarking visit, make certain to allot adequate time for them to talk one-on-one with their counterparts in the benchmark company. Listening to formal presentations and going on facility tours will not give them enough of the specifics that they will be looking for. The most valuable time they can spend is talking frankly with their peers. Most likely, you will need to coach your own executives before the visit, encouraging them to ask questions such as What do you personally do differently? How are the activities that you spend time on today different from those you spent time on in the past? It is helpful to give your executives a previsit packet that includes a summary of the company background, pertinent company information, and an agenda that they can review prior to the visit. The better your executives are prepared, the more they will get out of the time spent at another company.

If you've ever taken a class, been tutored, or taken lessons to learn to play an instrument or a sport, you realize the importance of expert feedback. Having the teacher or coach observe you and comment on what you are doing correctly or incorrectly can actually help you to improve. We are not aware of most of the mistakes we make when we are trying something new until someone points them out to us and shows us the correct way to perform. Coaching that involves monitoring and ongoing feedback is critical until we acquire enough skill to monitor our own behavior and coach ourselves.

When first trying to implement new styles of management or leadership, your leaders will need coaching and feedback, too. If no one lets them know how they are doing, there is no way for them to know whether they need to make any changes or modifications. They will continue believing that they are doing the right thing because no one has corrected them. As we all know, this assumption is not necessarily accurate. If you think that your management team is having trouble changing its behavior because it lacks feedback, here are some actions that can help improve the situation.

Leaders do not receive adequate feedback on their behavior

- Implement a coaching or mentoring program.

- Develop formal measures that assess how well executive behavior is aligned with the company's vision and values.

Implement a Coaching or Mentoring Program

Often the executives possess the skills needed for a more participative approach to leadership. The reason their behavior is rarely consistent with this management style is that they do not recognize things they do that are inconsistent with the vision and values of the company. In fact, a lack of feedback, rather than a lack of skill, is often the cause of problems. Executives are simply not aware of situations where they make decisions or engage in actions that send the wrong message to employees. The only way to make them aware of these inconsistencies is to provide feedback on their behavior. One company implemented a coaching program to help ensure that the necessary feedback occurs. Senior executives gave feedback to their direct reports when they observed behavior or decision making that was inconsistent with the company's new approach to leadership, and the direct reports gave feedback to their bosses as well. The trick is to create a nonthreatening atmosphere for giving feedback, especially when a subordinate has to give it to his or her boss. It took a while for the directors to feel comfortable giving feedback to their bosses; this was illustrated by the mostly positive feedback that came back at first. Over time, subordinates became comfortable in providing corrective feedback, and by coaching each other, the executives in the top two layers of the organization were able to dramatically change their management style. For more information on executive coaching or mentoring, see *Flight of the Buffalo* by Ralph Stayer and James Belasco.

Develop Formal Measures That Assess How Well Executive Behavior Is Aligned with the Company's Vision and Values

To supplement the individualized feedback that executives give to each other or receive from their employees, some organizations formally measure the extent to which executive behavior is consistent with the vision and values. For example, part of one company's vision is that executives need to be in touch with their employees, their customers, and their key suppliers. This company requires executives to keep track of how much time they spend with internal and external customers, with key suppliers, and with employees in the plant or the service delivery areas. Executives are measured on performance factors that encourage alignment with the corporate vision. To supplement the data collected from executives, they also ask employees to evaluate the extent to which executive/management behavior is consistent with the company's vision and values. This question is asked on employee morale or climate surveys every six months. Responses to this question provide an overall assessment of how all senior executives walk the talk.

Assessments should not stop at the executive level. All senior managers and managers need to behave in ways that are consistent with the vision and values. Measures and employee assessment are just as critical at these levels as they are at the executive level. Data should be monitored, fed back to individual managers, and reviewed with superiors to determine if changes or modifications in behavior are necessary. Plans should be developed that outline ways for managers to get coaching or training, if needed, so that they are able to develop the skills they need to make the transition to the new management style.

℞

The reason that change initiatives fail in many organizations is that they are too far reaching and the time lines are too long. New initiatives cause additional work and change, which often result in organizational turmoil in the short run. Employees are told that they will see the benefits of their work, but many are skeptical, having gone along with other programs that consumed valuable resources without producing any lasting value for the organization. The long-term rewards touted are not immediate or certain, so they do not really exert a great amount of influence on employee behavior. In these cases, incentives or consequences are needed to shape employee behavior.

A good number of employees in any organization will always buy in to the change programs and devote time and effort to making them work without the threat of negative consequences. These individuals perceive that the long-term benefits to the organization and to them personally are worth the effort. Their focus on long-term benefits rather than the short-term pain allows them to see, in bigger terms, what the change can do for the organization. If you believe that incentives or consequences are needed to shape behavior in your organization, review the actions presented in this section.

Lack of planned positive or negative consequences

- Select individuals for top jobs whose behavior is consistent with the vision and values.

- Ask individuals who refuse to change to leave the organization.

- Link key behavioral measures to executive compensation.

Select Individuals for Top Jobs Whose Behavior Is Consistent with the Vision and Values

A major trucking firm helped change management behavior by promoting individuals whose leadership style was consistent with the company's new vision and values. Managers whose results were good but whose management style was autocratic did not get promoted. This approach sent a powerful message to managers: If you're interested in holding a leadership position in this company, it is important that your leadership style be characterized by participation, empowerment, and teamwork.

Although this approach is a powerful way to teach managers that leadership style is an important criterion for being promoted, it often takes several years for the message to get through to people. At first, managers are reluctant to believe that leadership style is an important factor in being promoted. If the organization consistently promotes managers with the approved leadership style and does not reward the undesirable style, eventually the message gets through; those who want to be promoted adjust their management style.

Ask Individuals Who Refuse to Change to Leave the Organization

With training, coaching, and positive incentives, most managers will learn to adapt to the new culture and gradually change their leadership style. In fact, most managers really want to do what is best for the organization and their employees and will change when necessary. However, a small percentage of managers cannot or will not change. They may have gotten to where they are by tightly controlling all of the activities in their domain and using an autocratic leadership style; now they refuse to change the style that has worked for them. Individuals who flatly refuse to change need to be removed from management positions or from the organization. If they are allowed to stay, everyone else gets the message that it is not essential to embrace the desired change.

The problem with this approach is that you may lose or alienate people with years of experience who are effective managers in other respects. Naturally, the company is reluctant to let go of valuable experience. In some cases, a binding employment contract may force you to relocate the person to a management position. Managers that refuse to change have a problem with their belief systems, not just their behavior. They just don't believe that effective management is characterized by things like trust, empowerment, and sharing information.

You will also encounter managers who want to change, but just can't seem do so. These individuals may have many years of experience and have a very difficult time translating their desire to change to the needed change in behavior. Deciding how to proceed with these employees is difficult. You need to make certain that you have provided ample training and coaching opportunities for these employees and enough feedback, with the appropriate consequences for nonperformance, so that they know where they stand. Having done all that, if you believe that an individual just cannot change, your best action may be to help the person find another job or offer him or her an early retirement package.

(Please note that your human resources department must be part of the performance feedback process and, if necessary, the eventual termination. You must follow all human resources guidelines to ensure that your organization does not expose itself unnecessarily to a potential lawsuit for wrongful termination or discrimination.)

Link Key Behavioral Measures to Executive Compensation

If you want to encourage people to behave in certain ways, reward the behavior. IBM, Federal Express, AT&T, and a number of other successful organizations link executive bonuses to measures of employee satisfaction. They reward executives for creating an environment where employees are treated fairly, are informed, and have a voice in the organization. At Federal Express, all employees are evaluated by their subordinates or teammates. The Federal Express bonus system is based on three factors: people (employees), service (customers), and profit (shareholders). The rating an employee receives from teammates and/or direct reports is so important that a low score prevents an individual from receiving any bonus, even if customer satisfaction and profit results are strong.

The key to making this approach work is to select the right behaviors to measure. One company linked the number of hours per week that executives spent in the plant to bonuses as a way to determine executive involvement with day-to-day operations and the employees. The measure backfired because although the executives spent time in the plant, they mostly stood around and talked with each other. As you can see, it is important to establish measures that encourage the behaviors you want. Measures need to be reviewed periodically, and adjusted where necessary, to ensure that you are achieving the desired results.

PART II IMPLEMENTATION ISSUES

In the first part of this book, we discussed problems associated with an improper vision or strategy for future success. In this section we will review typical problems that occur when organizations attempt to implement change or improvement initiatives. Part II addresses the specific treatments, therapy, and diet/lifestyle modifications we will employ to achieve our goal of being healthy. Chapter 5 considers organizations that cannot decide upon their approach to performance improvement and instead try to focus on too many factors at once. Chapter 6 addresses organizations whose efforts at improvement are disjointed; implementation of improvement efforts has only caught on in a few pockets of the organization, or portions of the business have implemented their own unique approaches to improvement. Finally, Chapter 7 focuses on organizations that try to do too much too quickly. If the topics covered in one of these chapters sounds like a problem that you're having, turn to it for more information.

Approach	We do not have a coherent, systematic approach to performance improvement.	Chapter 5
Scope	Our change effort is not working because it is not being implemented uniformly across the organization.	Chapter 6
Pace	We are trying to change too much too quickly, or we are getting started too late and doing too little.	Chapter 7

5 Approach

We do not have a coherent, systematic approach to performance improvement.

When we are sick, we go to doctors so that they can diagnose our problem and prescribe a course of treatment to rid our bodies of the illness. We expect our doctor to have a coherent, systematic approach to treating the illness. For example, if on our first visit the doctor prescribes one antibiotic and on the second visit one week later we are no better, so he or she prescribes something different, we get the feeling that the doctor is just hoping that something will work. If on the third visit we are still no better and the doctor switches medicine again, many patients will start to believe that the doctor may not know how to solve the problem. Perhaps it is time to switch physicians.

People in organizations are no different. They want to see a systematic approach to both work and improvement efforts. A scattered approach to improvement sends the message that management really doesn't know what it is doing. Now if management doesn't know what it's doing, why should the employees spend any amount of effort working on programs that may not have any value? In this chapter of the book, we will examine why some companies lack a systematic approach to improvement and suggest actions to help you build a cohesive approach to improvement for your organization. To begin your search, review the symptoms listed in the chart that follows and identify the most likely cause of your difficulties.

Symptoms

People are confused about how different initiatives relate to one another. (1)

Duplicate improvement work is going on in different parts of the organization. (1)

People are jaded because of past "failures." (1, 2)

People are so busy making improvements that the core work isn't getting done. (3)

It seems like the organization always has a "program of the year." Once the year is over, you never hear about it again. (2, 3)

Causes

1. No coordination between individual initiatives or programs.

2. History of going from one management program to another.

3. The number of initiatives is overwhelming, leaving little time for other work.

Now turn to the cause that seems to be the most likely source of your problem.

1. No Coordination between Individual Initiatives or Programs

When you look at the number of different performance improvement initiatives that are in place in many companies today, it is no wonder that employees are confused. ISO 9000, SPC, reengineering, activity-based costing, strategic planning, Baldrige assessments, and a number of other programs are often going on at the same time. Part of the reason that this situation is confusing to employees is that many of the initiatives seem to overlap or even contradict each other. Take for example this story of the superintendent of a major chemical company who once yelled at the plant manager in frustration, "Last week it was SPC; this week it's empowerment; next week it's diversity training. I thought we were doing TQM!" If he was confused, imagine how the employees felt. In this section, we will discuss four actions that you can take to achieve better integration and synergy across the performance improvement efforts in your organization.

No coordination between individual initiatives or programs

- Coordinate all initiatives under a single executive.

- Relate all initiatives to an overall model or framework, such as the Baldrige criteria.

- Link all improvement initiatives to your key goals or success factors.

- Develop a five-year implementation plan for various initiatives.

Coordinate All Initiatives under a Single Executive

One of the reasons that various performance improvement efforts in companies are disjointed is that different individuals lead them. The vice president of finance leads the activity-based costing initiative, the vice president of human resources leads the empowerment and high-performance work-systems effort, the director of quality heads up the Baldrige assessment, and plant-level quality managers lead the drive to become ISO certified. This arrangement naturally leads to conflicting priorities and confusion. Employees end up spending many hours each week attending meetings associated with these initiatives and have little time left to perform their regular job responsibilities. Since the work still has to get done, employees must shoulder increased responsibility and obligations in schedules that are typically full to begin with. With little coordination, employees wind up feeling frustrated as they try to meet all of the organizational demands.

The other problem with uncoordinated initiatives is that a great deal of work may be duplicated in pockets of the organization. Good ideas usually spring up throughout an organization in response to problems. Teams form to identify and implement new processes, programs, or other solutions. The key is to eliminate duplication of efforts by sharing what has been accomplished and learned with the rest of the organization. Coordination rarely occurs, so at any one time you may find several groups of people working on solutions to similar problems. Duplication is a real waste of the resources (people, time, and money) of an organization.

To put an end to the madness, or prevent it from occurring in the first place, some forward-thinking organizations coordinate all performance improvement efforts under a single executive. The executive serves as the overall project manager for organizational improvement, similar to a general contractor on a building project. Thus, the executive can screen for unnecessary or redundant initiatives, serve as a guide for the projects, and also be a watchdog to ensure that the programs are moving forward and achieving positive results for the organization. Another important responsibility that this executive has is to ensure that no one individual or unit within the organization is taxed too heavily by responsibilities for performance improvement initiatives. Responsibility should be distributed throughout the organization so that it does not cripple a single unit or individual. For further information, see "Appoint a Process Owner" in Chapter 9.

Relate All Initiatives to an Overall Model or Framework, such as the Baldrige Criteria

One way to make sense of the confusing array of programs and initiatives is to frame everything around a comprehensive model or system for looking at organizations and their performance. The most widely accepted model for doing this is the criteria from the Malcolm Baldrige National Quality Award. What started out in 1988 as an award for companies that did a good job controlling quality and satisfying customers has evolved into a model for effectively running an organization. The Baldrige Award criteria are not just for business; they have also been adapted for health care and educational organizations. The seven categories and associated items in the criteria provide a framework for categorizing and organizing all the different performance improvement initiatives you have in progress.

Two very successful companies that use this model to coordinate their improvement efforts are Cargill and Air Products and Chemicals. Cargill, an agricultural company, is one of the largest privately owned businesses, with 70,000 employees worldwide. Air Products is a $3 billion dollar company that produces gases and chemicals for a variety of industries. Both companies use and teach the Baldrige Award criteria as the overall structure in which to categorize all their performance improvement efforts. This approach has been very successful for these two companies because it allows employees to see the big picture. When learning about individual initiatives such as reengineering or ISO 9000 certification, employees learn where each fits in the overall Baldrige framework. For additional information on the Baldrige Award criteria and how they can be used to organize improvement activities, see *Baldrige Award Winning Quality* by Mark Graham Brown.

Link All Improvement Initiatives to Your Key Goals or Success Factors

Another way to make sense of the array of change programs and improvement initiatives in your organization is to link them all to your major goals or to your key success factors. By establishing the link to organizational goals, initiatives are undertaken only when they *clearly* contribute to future success. Goals also provide a logical framework for organizing the initiatives. One organization that has done this extremely well is Pacific Bell's Shared Services function. Shared Services is an organization of approximately 1000 employees that provides procurement, real estate, logistics, safety, and other types of support services to the corporation. Shared Services links all improvement initiatives to the organization's Four Priorities: (1) customer satisfaction, (2) cost reduction, (3) job fulfillment, and (4) process improvement. All initiatives, programs, and individual improvement projects must be tied directly to one or more of the Four Priorities to provide order and structure to their improvement efforts.

Develop a Five-Year Implementation Plan for Various Initiatives

To coordinate a myriad of initiatives and programs that are ongoing or slated to begin in your organization, develop a detailed project plan with a time line that outlines exactly when each initiative will be implemented, how long it will run, how much of the organization's resources it will consume, and so on. This is no small task, but it is certainly worthwhile to get a realistic picture of how much the organization should be undertaking at any one time. To begin, categorize the initiatives as a basic, intermediate, or advanced level of change, indicating any projects that may be precursors to others or higher priorities to the organization. For example, ISO 9000 certification is a good foundation upon which to build other quality initiatives. It should be done prior to performing a full-blown Baldrige assessment and improvement plan. Other initiatives may be conducted simultaneously because of their complementary nature. For example, in a process reengineering program, benchmarking is often conducted to learn about the best practices of other organizations prior to implementing a new process. Then map out all the initiatives or programs on a five-year planning grid. Once that is complete, you can develop a strategy that makes sense for the organization. The plan will help you see what the organization can undertake now and in the future, and may cause you to shift programs because of the resource constraints of the organization. For more information on determining which types of initiatives should be done at the various stages of your overall improvement effort, see

"Quality: Small and Midsized Companies Seize the Challenge—Not a Moment Too Soon" by Otis Port.

It is no wonder that employees in many companies are skeptical when management announces a new program that will solve all the company's problems. Many have seen a dozen or so of these programs come and go in their careers and are not fazed by the announcement of yet another. Others, (those newer to the organization) may believe that the new program will really fix the organization's problems. It is a well-documented fact that business organizations are guilty of looking for a quick fix to solve their problems. Many waste thousands, even millions of dollars, going from program to program.

A program gets dropped when the work becomes difficult or when something that sounds easier and more appealing comes along. If yours is an organization that is guilty of this "program-of-the-month" mentality, review the actions below; one may help put you on the right course for change and keep you there for the duration.

History of going from one management program to another

- Do not trust the promise of quick results.
- Do your homework before selecting an improvement approach.
- Develop your own change or improvement initiative rather than adopting someone else's.

Do Not Trust the Promise of Quick Results

 One way to halt your organization's continual search for a new panacea is to avoid any consultant or program that promises to fix all of the problems in your organization in a year or two. Changing your corporate culture or reengineering your major processes is not a one- to two-year project, and anyone touting change in that time frame is not being honest with you. Many companies such as Xerox, Chrysler, Ford, Corning, and Miliken have completely changed their cultures and caused dramatic turnarounds in quality and financial results; however, none of them accomplished the change without five to ten years worth of extremely hard work. If you have the opportunity, listen to executives from organizations who have dramatically improved their performance. They will give you first-hand accounts of the amount of work, effort, and sacrifice required to make an organizational change of that magnitude.

Another way to prevent the "program-of-the-month" approach in your organization is to spend the time finding an approach that will work for your company and putting together a realistic implementation plan. Not all plans will work for all organizations. Some organizations are smaller and more nimble by nature, willing to embrace changes that come along; others have an older culture that needs to change more slowly so that everyone embraces the change and no one feels threatened. Even more important, once you find the right approach, stick with it for however long it takes to achieve the desired improvements. Beware of the tendency to drop the program after the first couple of years. This is when the work gets difficult and when dramatic improvements become less prevalent. For more information on how to avoid the quick-fix mentality in your company, consult *Beyond the Quick Fix* by Ralph Kilmann.

Do Your Homework before Selecting an Improvement Approach

  The key to avoiding a never-ending search for the one program that will really change or revolutionize your organization is to do your homework before selecting an approach. Many organizations have had a great deal of success implementing and successfully maintaining a TQM change effort. Federal Express, Motorola, and 3M are among successful, respected companies that have spent many years making TQM part of their organizational cultures. Others, like FMC Corporation of Chicago, have focused on the "balanced scoreboard" approach to improve organizational performance. (See the articles by Robert Kaplan and David Norton.) Reengineering efforts have been employed in other organizations. All of these approaches to improving organizational performance have their merits and have produced positive results for companies. However, for every success story, you can find just as many failures. Failure is not often caused by the chosen approach but by the implementation and lack of follow-through.

The key to finding an improvement approach that works for your organization is to find one that can remedy an organizational problem and, at the same time, fit with your current practices, values, and culture. Therefore, it is important to spend time investigating all approaches being considered. Do research, talk to other companies that have implemented a similar program, and talk to consulting firms that assist organizations with planning and implementation before settling on an approach for your organization. Consider selecting an approach that has worked for other companies in your industry. The following chart provides a framework for beginning your research into organizational improvement programs.

Strategy	Rewards	People	Systems	Measures
TQM	Gainsharing	Self-directed work teams	Activity-based costing	Balanced scorecard
Reengineering	Skill-based pay			
Strategic realignment		Quality-improvement teams	Process improvement	Performance-based measures
		Curriculum development		

TQM is the most comprehensive of all the performance improvement approaches in that it focuses on fundamental changes in all aspects of how the organization runs. It also has the best empirical evidence of success. Winners of the Baldrige Award, for example, tend to outperform other companies in the stock market. For additional information on selecting the best approach for performance improvement, consult *Why TQM Fails and What to Do about It* by Brown, Hitchcock, and Willard.

Develop Your Own Change or Improvement Initiative Rather Than Adopting Someone Else's

An organization can avoid the program-of-the-month syndrome by developing its own change or improvement initiative. Organizations that have purchased programs from a consultant or another company often find that the package doesn't quite fit their culture. For example, agricultural giant Cargill had trouble implementing a consulting organization's approach in its European businesses. The program was not only seen as too American but also seen as too heavily oriented to manufacturing. Cargill has since developed its own unique approach to quality improvement that is specific to its business and culture. Cargill still retains the consulting organization, but it now develops customized improvement initiatives and training materials for the corporation. Cargill, like many others, has found that a home-grown approach makes it much less likely that improvement initiatives will be shelved every few years in favor of the newest approach being touted by industry consultants.

3. The Number of Initiatives Is Overwhelming, Leaving Little Time for Other Work

Most organizations are very lean today. The fat has been trimmed and the surviving employees often have to accept a significant amount of additional responsibilities. It is not unusual for most professionals or managers to put in 10 to 50 percent more hours than a standard work week. Employees in these organizations naturally resist performance improvement initiatives, like TQM and reengineering, because they have too much on their plates already. There is no shift or elimination of duties, just additional responsibilities delegated. When employees challenge their superiors about how to handle their existing workloads and participate in performance improvement initiatives, management often responds with trite phrases like: You need to do a better job prioritizing your activities, or Work smarter, not harder. The reality is that something will not get done. Either the workload must be analyzed and redistributed or time spent on performance improvement initiatives needs to be limited. Review the recommended actions listed on the next page to assist you in achieving a better balance between work and initiatives.

The number of initiatives is overwhelming, leaving little time for other work

- Eliminate unnecessary or redundant initiatives or programs.
- Limit time spent on performance improvement initiatives.

Eliminate Unnecessary or Redundant Initiatives or Programs

Since the day-to-day work cannot be eliminated, unnecessary improvement programs must go. Many large organizations have far too many improvement initiatives being worked on in pockets throughout the organization. These organizations try to accomplish too much in a limited time frame. The motives are noble as organizations scramble for survival or try to stay one step ahead of the competition. However, the bottom line is that when resources are stretched as far as they can go, some of these initiatives need to be eliminated or combined. The following steps outline a systematic process for analysis and reduction of redundant programs.

1. Prepare a matrix that lists all the individual initiatives (e.g., ISO 9000 certification of a plant, benchmarking your billing and invoicing process, improving the response-center time) down the left side of the chart and the areas for improvement (e.g., cost reduction, improvement in customer satisfaction, process improvement) along the top of the chart. The matrix will graphically depict the amount of overlap you might have in your programs or initiatives.

2. Get a full description of each initiative including the scope of the project, the goals, the intended duration, and the resource requirements. Find out what stage the project is in.

3. Charter a team to review all of the data collected, conduct any additional investigations needed, and determine which initiatives can be eliminated or combined. The team may be made up of those leading some of the initiatives, but you need to be aware that people have a tendency to protect their own programs. To make this process work, the executive running the meetings should be responsible for all improvement initiatives and be able to facilitate a consensus on how and where programs can be eliminated or reduced in scope.

Limit Time Spent on Performance Improvement Initiatives

Some employees like to be involved in committees and teams that work on improving the performance of the organization. Others find these activities boring and frustrating, feeling that teams often belabor the details and take forever to reach consensus on issues and accomplish tasks. The organization tends to call on the same people repeatedly to participate in improvement initiatives—those who are willing and enthusiastic. The employees who like to work on committees and teams often end up spending 10 to 50 percent of their time each week in these improvement initiative meetings, leaving little time to meet their other responsibilities.

One way to prevent or correct this problem is to establish guidelines for time spent on improvement activities. For example, one large corporation suggests that all employees, regardless of level or function, spend an average of 24 hours a month participating in activities designed to improve the performance of the organization. Time spent on these activities is tracked so that employees don't spend too much or too little time on improvement initiatives. The trick is for your organization to determine the average number of hours each employee should be spending on improvement programs and to institute a measurement and consequence system to promote the desired behavior.

6 Scope

Our change effort is not working because it is not being implemented uniformly across the organization.

In Chapter Five we talked about having the correct approach to improving performance. In this chapter we will focus on issues related to having too many approaches. Diversity is good and needs to be encouraged, to a point. Take, for example, patients in the hospital. Over the course of the day, they see different nurses as shifts change. However, patient care has to be uniform to ensure that the patients are properly medicated, that they are fed, that records are properly kept, that all patients receive the appropriate tests, and so on. There are standards or procedures for care that are typically uniform in a particular institution. Now having standards does not mean every nurse becomes an automaton performing these tasks, but it does mean that each one understands the level of care expected and adapts his or her behavior to provide that level of care.

The same thing needs to happen in an organization if it is to make any lasting changes. Everyone in the organization has to embrace the change in a uniform fashion to allow the change to become part of the fabric of the organization. Allowing each location or unit within an organization to adopt its own approach to improving performance can cause confusion and waste resources. In this situation, units often adopt the "not invented here" mentality, and any programs or efforts for finding synergies across units are lost. If your change effort is not working simply because the program is being implemented autonomously in many different parts of the organization, review the symptoms listed in the chart that follows and identify the most likely cause of your difficulties.

Symptoms

Some locations or units are not participating in the change or improvement initiative. (1)

Employees who transfer in from other locations or units express confusion regarding the new unit's improvement effort. (2)

There are no perceived consequences for lack of participation in the improvement effort. (1)

A large number of consulting firms appear to be working on various programs in units throughout the organization. (2)

Each business unit or location conducts its programs autonomously with little cooperation or dialogue across boundaries. (2)

Causes

1. The company does not or will not mandate participation in the change initiative.

2. Different business units or locations use inconsistent approaches.

Now turn to the cause which seems to be the most likely source of your problem.

1. The Company Does Not or Will Not Mandate Participation in the Change Initiative

Some companies have a very hands-off approach to managing their business units or remote locations. Unlike McDonald's, which tightly controls the operations at each franchise location, some organizations prefer to let each business unit or location handle its own operations as long as it is profitable. Johnson & Johnson, with hundreds of small business units, used this approach to maintain an entrepreneurial spirit in the business units and avoid much of the typical large-corporation bureaucracy. The problem with this type of approach is that when you try to implement a change effort such as TQM or reengineering, it is tough to sell the program throughout the corporation.

A major manufacturer of power tools and small appliances spent three years trying to convince management in its various business units of the benefits of conducting a Baldrige assessment as a way to uncover areas that need improvement. Only a few business units were willing to attend the corporate-sponsored training and complete the assessment; most were reluctant to make any commitment to the program. The units that refused to participate were the ones that were the least customer focused. They viewed the program as just another activity that would waste time and distract them from the bottom-line results they were driven to produce each quarter. After failing to convince the CEO to mandate the assessment and improvement plans, the vice president of quality resigned in frustration. (The organization failed to show any progress toward becoming more customer focused in all but a few of its business units.)

If you feel that your company is not supportive of the change initiative or program(s), review the actions listed below for a solution to your difficulties.

The company does not or will not mandate participation in the change initiative

- Sell upper management on requiring units/locations to implement basic action plans.

- Develop a marketing strategy to sell the benefits to business units or locations.

- Develop recognition programs to reward business units or locations that excel.

Sell Upper Management on Requiring Units/Locations to Implement Basic Action Plans

The best way to convince management to mandate participation in a change initiative is to provide it with data on the cost of the effort and the company's lack of progress toward its goal(s). Chances are that the company has already made a large investment of time and money to create and conduct training for all of the business units on the change initiative. Executives probably assume that all of the units are at least trying to implement the initiative in stages, but that may not be so. Many units may appear to be going along with the program without actually making any substantive changes. Once executives are confronted with the lack of progress, they may be willing to take more forceful action to ensure that the corporate investment pays off. A word of caution: Do be careful presenting the information on the lack of business unit participation as your report may be perceived as finger pointing. It may be better to use a consultant to present this information.

Senior executives can also benefit from knowing what other leading companies have done and why their initiatives have made them successful. Focus particularly on the strategic implementation of the initiative across their organizations. As you can see, you must sometimes paint the picture that people need to be forced to do what is right. If each business unit is left to decide how and when to implement a transformation initiative, many will not take the time to do it. NYNEX has an effective approach to obtain participation in the company's Baldrige assessment and improvement effort. Each business unit or loca-

tion is required to complete an assessment, but it can choose from three separate approaches, which range from a simple, inexpensive assessment to a thorough, and more resource intensive, assessment. Another international telecommunications company uses a similar approach in that it requires each business to use the criteria from its country's quality award to complete an annual evaluation and improvement plan.

Develop a Marketing Strategy to Sell the Initiatives to Business Units or Locations

If you cannot convince senior management to mandate participation in a change initiative, the only option is to sell the business units or locations on the idea and get voluntary participation. Many organizations do a poor job of marketing their improvement programs or change initiatives. They often believe that the units or locations should recognize that cooperating with the program can only be to their benefit and wonder what there really is to sell. While it may be true that each unit will derive a benefit from the change, it many not be apparent. What is often apparent is the resource commitment required for training and implementation.

The other obstacle you will be working against is skepticism that this program is yet another in a long line of programs that has come to the forefront and then quietly disappeared—perhaps the same old thing with a new label. This prevailing attitude is unlikely to generate much enthusiasm or interest in your business units or locations. Consequently, you must put together an effective marketing strategy. You will need to convince business unit managers of a number of things:

1. The program is really new and different from what they've seen in the past.

2. The organization will benefit from implementing the program.

3. The implementation will be fairly simple and will not disrupt operations.

Ford Parts & Service (FP&S) does an outstanding job of marketing its change efforts. FP&S distributes to independent dealers who sell and repair Ford cars. Ford cannot mandate that these dealers implement any particular program or improvement initiative, yet over the last ten years, it has been able to implement a number of very successful initiatives designed to improve service quality. The programs have been successful because of their good designs and effective marketing strategies. Ford spends as much money on the marketing effort as it spends on program development. FP&S personnel travel through the country, holding regional preview sessions to introduce dealers to new programs and get them to participate in the programs. Ford must demonstrate real value to these dealers who must pay to participate in the programs.

Here are some very simple rules to follow to successfully market your change initiative or transformation programs:

• Design the program specifically for the organization implementing it—do not use an off-the-shelf approach that may not fit.

• Package the program simply—concentrate on visual appeal.

• Keep the cost of the program low so that everyone can afford to participate.

• Concentrate on a few practical steps that can be taken to improve performance. Do not espouse theory or offer a wide variety of approaches.

• Concentrate on presenting the features and benefits of the program in all marketing materials.

Develop Recognition Programs to Reward Business Units or Locations That Excel

In 1990 a leading trucking and transportation firm decided to adopt a quality framework for changing the culture of its company. An effort to interest its distribution centers in using the quality criteria to improve their businesses was less than successful. In this case, a marketing pitch was not the answer either. Rather than force locations to do the assessments, or try to sell them on the benefits of assessing performance and identifying areas that needed improvement, the company created an award to recognize those locations that excelled. Named after the company founder, the award has been an effective catalyst for change in the company. Over the five-year period, the award gained recognition, and the business locations showed more interest in learning about the quality criteria, conducting assessments, and instituting improvements. The award appealed to the fact that people like recognition for their efforts. In addition, the company began promoting those managers whose units or locations won the award rather than promoting managers in nonwinning locations.

Other organizations have adopted internal quality-award programs. Rather than encouraging business units to compete against each other for a few coveted prizes, these organizations set no limits on the number of winners. Awards are based on reaching certain score levels.

If you want to develop an award system, the following simple rules may help ensure success:
- Offer multiple awards to discourage competitiveness between internal business units.

- Make certain the program has executive commitment and backing.

- Publicize and market the award.

- Do not make the award so difficult to achieve that no one can possibly win; on the other hand, if it is too easy to attain, no one will take it seriously.

- Make certain that the winners are recognized and rewarded and that others identify the winners as an example to be followed.

Many large organizations today are quite diverse and operate various businesses in a number of very different industries. TRW, for example, is in three distinct businesses: automotive, aerospace/defense, and credit reporting. When the parent company decides to adopt a particular approach, it often does not make sense to mandate the same approach for all parts of its business. Allowing each business or business unit to develop its own approach with accountability to the parent organization is a popular methodology used for implementing a new improvement initiative. Although business managers are usually comfortable with designing their own approach or adapting the corporate model, resources are wasted when each business unit reinvents the wheel. Having a variety of approaches to performance improvement also tends to encourage the company to function as a collection of separate businesses rather than as one team. Companies such as IBM, American Express, and Northrop-Grummon have been rewarded for working hard to develop a unified approach that all units in the organization can implement. Moving the whole organization in the same direction fosters commonality of purpose, achieves synergies across units, and creates momentum. If you feel that your company is inconsistent in its approach to change or improvement initiatives, here are several techniques that you can use.

Inconsistent approaches used in different business units or locations

- Develop a model that requires standardization of key aspects of the approach—but also allows customization.

- Provide standardized training to all locations/units in the organization.

- Develop a customized approach for each area of the organization.

Develop a Model That Requires Standardization of Key Aspects of the Approach—but Also Allows Customization

 A number of big organizations refuse to mandate change programs in their business units or locations for fear that they will lose the "small business feel" that comes from being able to operate somewhat autonomously. One downside of this philosophy is variability in the extent to which a change effort, such as TQM, has been implemented. In big corporations and government organizations, you can often find parts of the organization that are world class and other parts that have not even begun the transformation effort.

One organization that has done well at standardizing its approach to organizational transformation is the U.S. Air Force. The Air Force's goal has been to become more customer focused. Although different Air Force bases vary widely in how far they have progressed in their TQM implementation, they all follow a standardized approach called the Air Force Quality Award Criteria. Each base around the world is required to complete an assessment against the criteria. This assessment is used to identify problem areas that require improvement plans. The criteria, which are similar to the Baldrige Award criteria, give each base the opportunity to interpret and apply the standards as it deems appropriate.

The benefit of a standardized model that allows for customization is that, at a minimum, all of the businesses or business units have reviewed the general areas in which the company wants to focus its improvement efforts and they know the overall standards that they should be striving to attain. Their strengths and weaknesses may be very different from organization to organization, but each unit must work to attain the same basic goals. The road each unit takes will vary, but the end result should be an entire organization that has instituted and embraced necessary change.

Provide Standardized Training to All Locations/Units in the Organization

   Large, diverse organizations that have had the most success with their change or improvement efforts typically have adopted a standardized training approach to teach all of their units or locations about the improvement program. In the 1980s, when quality improvement first became a concern, training was much less available and often less formal than it is now. If managers were sent to a quality school, such as Phil Crosby Associates Quality College in Florida, they might have been responsible for passing their new found knowledge on to the rest of the organization upon their return. Today, companies know that they must select a standardized approach to training, whether the training is developed internally or purchased from an outside provider, and they must provide across-the-board learning opportunities for all employees if a change or quality-improvement initiative is to work.

Does this mean that you must mandate certain training or workshops for different target audiences throughout your organization? In many cases it does. Appleton Papers, a Wisconsin-based company that produces carbonless paper, has successfully standardized the leadership and quality improvement training it uses in all of its facilities. Appleton decided to develop its own curriculum and course materials to implement the approach it calls "customer-focused quality." This plan gave Appleton the flexibility to incorporate the latest thinking from top management gurus and develop courses that were appropriate for all levels of employees throughout the organization. The program was delivered to all of the paper mills, and the approach has been extremely successful for the company, as it has achieved full participation in the program. Appleton's organization is now driven to achieve customer-focused quality. Its success is evidenced by the fact that Appleton Papers was a finalist for the Malcolm Baldrige National Quality Award in 1994, the first year it submitted an application.

Providing standardized training does mean that every person in the organization gets the *same* training. It means that the organization is providing training on a single approach rather than a myriad of disjointed approaches. It also means that every person in the organization has the opportunity to learn about the program and be shown practical ways to apply the changes to his or her work environment. Quite a bit of customization of the training materials may be necessary to adapt them for the different target-audience groups throughout the organization. Skilled instructional designers can help your organization design and develop training to fit the needs of all of the target audiences throughout your organization.

Develop a Customized Approach for Each Area of the Organization

Organizations tend to be uneven in their deployment of change efforts. Change is often initiated where it will have the most impact on customer satisfaction and the corporate bottom line. Those areas tend to be the manufacturing or the service delivery areas of the business—where the processes are more definitive and the improvements have a tangible impact on profitability. Companies develop programs to improve or initiate change efforts in these areas, but when it comes to the administrative or support functions (e.g., finance or human resources), they often have difficulty adapting what they have done in other parts of the organization. In general, administrative or support areas lag in the implementation of change initiatives.

This divergence points out the need for a customized approach to implementing an initiative throughout the organization. Rather than trying to make a program or initiative that was designed for the factory or service delivery area appropriate for the support areas, a unique approach might make more sense. The basic philosophies of change can remain constant throughout the organization because goals such as focus on prevention or delighting customers have universal application. The uniqueness comes in the approach. The support functions, for example, often have different groups of customers—some may be internal and others external to the organization—whose needs conflict. Some support functions have a captive audience, so their customers have no choice but to use their services. *Service Within* by Karl Albrecht provides sound advice on the unique nature of implementing improvement initiatives in support functions.

7 Pace

We are trying to change too much too quickly, or we are getting started too late and doing too little.

People often have unrealistic expectations about the pace at which they can change things. Those who start a new health or diet program get discouraged if they don't see results in a few days or few weeks. It is our nature to expect results immediately; after all, we are putting in a lot of effort! What is most difficult is determining the level of results that we can *realistically* expect and accepting the pace of change, which usually occurs more slowly than we would like. Failure most often occurs when expectations are not in line with reality and disappointment sets in. In our minds, change can occur much more quickly than it actually does; we forget to factor in the myriad of other demands and issues that we must face daily. Organizations must handle their day-to-day operations, which is often a challenge in itself, while they implement change programs. Because the organization is working with a limited resource base, the pace of change will not be as quick as management might like.

We also forget that old habits or patterns are hard to break. Return, for a moment, to the person starting a new health program who has decided to stop smoking, go on a diet, and begin a new exercise regime. All of these things will contribute to the goal of a healthful lifestyle. Although the goal is noble, there is a danger in trying to tackle too much at once. Efforts are not focused, and he or she may begin to feel overwhelmed and unable to keep up with all of the changes. Once that point is reached, frustration sets in and our health seeker gives up the program.

Since organizations are simply a collection of people, the same grappling with change occurs. When organizations want to change, often they believe that everything must be changed and changed now. They have the tendency to want to fix everything immediately rather than prioritize what needs to be done and put together a realistic plan for accomplishment. Organizations, like people, have to set realistic plans and goals so that they do not abandon an improvement program because it has become too much work.

72

Overall, the organization must determine a realistic level of change and then manage the expectations of those in the organization to alleviate frustration. If your change effort is not working because the pace of change is not right for the organization, review the symptoms listed in the chart that follows and identify the most likely cause of your difficulties.

Symptoms	Causes
Management is frustrated by the lack of change. (1)	1. Management has unreasonable expectations about what can be accomplished.
Company is losing market share. (2)	
Company is losing a number of key customers. (2)	2. Change efforts were not proactive and now must be reactive.
Company is facing more and more real competition each year. (2)	3. We are doing too little and are not making enough progress.
The change effort has lost focus and momentum. (3, 4)	4. Progress and results have plateaued.
People are discouraged and lack interest in the effort. (3,4)	5. The change program is not embraced because it was forced on the organization.
One or more key customers require process changes to continue a business relationship. (5)	

Now turn to the cause that seems to be the most likely source of your problem.

Rx 1. Management Has Unreasonable Expectations about What Can Be Accomplished

Often when senior management commits to a particular improvement initiative such as TQM, it wants to transform the company in a year or two. Managers may hear of the rewards gained by other organization's efforts and want the changes to occur quickly in their own. This enthusiasm for change should be harnessed and used, but in some cases it must be tempered a bit. Changing any organization takes time. The rule of thumb used by organizations that have implemented TQM efforts is to plan for one year of work for every layer of management in the organization. Even when executives hear the warning from other companies that change takes time, they often believe that their organization is different, that they can learn from the lessons and experience of others, and that they don't need to spend as much time as other companies have spent. If you feel that your management has unrealistic expectations about the change that can be accomplished in a given time frame, here are several approaches that you can use.

Management has unreasonable expectations about what can be accomplished

- Educate management on the pace of change results in organizations similar to your own.

- Challenge stretch goals by asking for relevant benchmarks.

Educate Management on the Pace of Change Results in Organizations Similar to Your Own

Once executives get excited about TQM, reengineering, or another improvement strategy, you want to channel that enthusiasm into the development of reasonable implementation plans. Executives need to be educated on the time, resource commitment, and effort required to implement an organizationwide change. The best way for them to understand what it takes is to listen to those who have already implemented change. Select organizations that are similar to your own in size and industry, who are perhaps five years ahead of you in their implementation of the change effort you favor, and set up site visits or corporate field trips to those organizations. Arrange for your executives to spend some time with their counterparts so they can discuss goals and implementation schedules.

The motive behind these corporate field trips is to teach your executives what to expect when trying to implement a change effort in your own company, not how other companies perform a particular process. The goal of these field trips is to get your executives to understand what is realistic and practical for an organization of your size to accomplish in a particular time frame. This understanding must then be translated into a set of realistic expectations and goals for the implementation of your own change effort. A good place to find companies to visit is the list of winners of the Malcolm Baldrige National Quality Award and/or the winners of state-level awards that are based on the Baldrige. Winners of these awards have proven that they are customer focused, have their processes under control, and embrace changes when necessary to improve the organization and service to customers. In addition, these companies are usually quite willing to accept visitors from other companies. For information on winners, contact the National Institute of Standards and Technology at (301) 975-2036.

Challenge Stretch Goals by Asking for Relevant Benchmarks

Win the state quality award in two years or charter process improvement teams in all plant processes this year are examples of stretch goals that executives may set without much thought as to how reasonable or achievable those goals might actually be. Stretch goals are an effective way to stimulate action and cause employees to rethink the way that they do their work. However, stretch goals should be based on research, not on a whim. One company instituted a stretch goal called "80 in 5," which meant that it wanted to achieve an 80 percent improvement on all measures in five years. The 80 percent and five years were both completely arbitrary. Not much thought had been given to the resources needed to achieve this goal and whether or not an 80 percent improvement on all performance measures was possible or desirable.

When management sets arbitrary stretch goals for the implementation of performance improvement initiatives, challenge those goals by asking what they are based on. A stretch goal should never be set without knowing where you are today and without enough fact finding and research that tells you if the goal is, in fact, achievable. In 1990, one company set a goal to win the Malcolm Baldrige Award by 1995. The CEO set this stretch goal without knowing where the company stood on the Baldrige scale and without realizing how much work it would take to win the award in five years. He was operating under the assumption that the company could begin its quest with a score of at least 500 points on the Baldrige scale because it had been working on TQM for four to five years. In fact, the company's score in 1990 was only 250/1000. This score meant that winning the award in five years was not a reasonable stretch goal for the organization.

To set a stretch goal, use the following steps:

1. Conduct a current assessment of organizational performance to understand where your organization is today.

2. Set the target or end goals of what you would like the organization to attain. Do not discuss time frames at this point.

3. Research/benchmark what other companies have done to achieve the goals you are attempting to achieve.

4. Develop a rough time-line and resource map to determine the investment required from the organization to achieve the established goal.

5. With a full understanding of the resources required to achieve a goal, set the stretch goal for the organization.

Like people who tend to procrastinate, organizations tend to put off doing things they know they should until it is too late. People who have said for years that they need to quit smoking develop lung cancer and emphysema. Organizations wait until they face a crisis before they get serious about changing the way they do business. Xerox did not really begin to change its organization until its Japanese competitors had severely eroded its market share. Ford and General Motors waited until it was almost too late before they made significant improvements in their quality and operational measures that enabled them to remain competitive in the automotive market. For every company like Ford and Xerox that has succeeded in a dramatic turnaround in the face of tough competition, there are many others that didn't make it. They waited too long and did too little to save their companies.

The good part about waiting too long is that it is easy to establish a sense of urgency. If the doctor tells you you're going to die in a year unless you dramatically change your lifestyle, you don't spend much time planning a strategy or making excuses—you change your lifestyle. The bad thing about waiting is that you have a lot of ground to cover and you have to work much harder to achieve the necessary results. Here are several approaches that your organization can use if it has waited too long to implement change.

Change efforts were not proactive and now must be reactive

- Identify and implement short-term survival strategies.
- Implement a fast-track action plan.

Identify and Implement Short-Term Survival Strategies

Organizations that have been successful in their implementation of TQM will tell you that one key to success is focusing on short-term victories. These organizations spend the first year to two years working on process improvements or solving problems that will produce short-term, dramatic improvements in key performance measures. This strategy is often referred to as picking the low-hanging fruit or going after the projects with the biggest bang for the buck. This approach is good for a company that wants to keep employees committed to a long-term change effort, but it will not work if you have waited too long to begin your change effort.

An organization that should have started its improvement efforts long ago must identify the short-term improvements that it needs to make in key areas. Start by analyzing the factors that have contributed to the downturn in your organization. Then select one or two key areas where you are failing, or where the competition is markedly ahead of you, and develop strategies to change or fix those areas quickly. For Xerox, the key area was product cost. Xerox had to figure out how to remove significant costs from its manufacturing and distribution process because the competition was selling copying machines for what it cost Xerox to manufacture its copier! The first thing that the American car companies had to fix was product quality. To their credit, they focused all of their efforts on improving the quality of their cars before they began to focus improvement efforts on the quality of service provided by dealers.

There is great danger in focusing on the wrong factors at this stage. If you do, you're dead. A number of companies have focused their improvement efforts around product quality in recent years, making dramatic improvements. Some found out too late that improvements in product quality did not increase their market share, revenue, or customer satisfaction. Spend the time necessary to analyze the market and your competitors thoroughly before determining the key areas in which you will concentrate your short-term improvement efforts. For more information on finding the right success strategy for your organization, consult *The Discipline of Market Leaders* by Michael Treacy and Fred Wiersema.

Implement a Fast-Track Action Plan

Another approach to employ if you waited too long to start your improvement effort is the fast-track approach. Organizational change programs typically involve a phased approach to implementation over a number of years, typically anywhere from three to ten years. Organizations that are under the gun do not have much time to spend changing their cultures or implementing an improvement effort. In this situation, the organization must implement several phases of an improvement effort concurrently. The keys to making the fast-track approach work are a sense of urgency, a commitment of resources, and a detailed project plan.

• Everyone needs to understand the need to make large-scale changes quickly in order for the organization to survive and prosper.

- Executives need to commit a number of key individuals to work on the change effort, and perhaps enlist the aid of outside consultants to lead the improvement initiative.

- The change effort requires a detailed design and implementation plan and a project manager who can coordinate the various efforts that will be part of the initiative.

The entire organization must understand the importance of the initiative and fully support the effort. Without that support and dedication, the organization may not survive.

One large federal government agency had been working on TQM implementation for almost 15 years and had made very little progress. The organization was still educating employees on statistical control and problem solving, but nothing had really changed in day-to-day operations. Most organizations experience some level of resistance to change. Organizations that are most resistant are typically the profitable, market leaders who feel a sense of security in that position. Organizations that have experienced the real possibility of demise have no problem getting everyone to commit to a change effort.

The toughest organizations to change are those that are successful. They may do some training, or other nonthreatening things, but they are often unwilling to make any real operational or process changes. The thought is, Why fix something if it isn't broken? It's difficult to get an organization with record profits to even think about doing business in a different way or to expend the effort needed to become world class in all areas. We all know that short-term profitability is no guarantee of long-term success, but the fact remains, the better an organization's results, the less likely it is to change. Here are a few approaches to use if it appears as though your organization does not intend to focus on change.

Lack of real commitment to and progress in the change effort

- Establish a sense of urgency for change.

- Engage an outside agency or consultant to help evaluate your progress and develop an action plan.

Establish a Sense of Urgency for Change

The biggest barrier to any change momentum is employees who do not perceive a threat from the competition and find no reason for the company to change. Employees at IBM used to feel that way. IBM was the market leader—with its competitors trailing far behind. IBM was the dominant force in the computer industry and experienced year after year of growth. All of that changed as the market began to erode. After laying off half the company, IBM is no longer complacent and unwilling to change. In the last three years, IBM has made major improvements in its processes, and it is on the way to achieving its vision of being a market-driven company.

Urgency is not a by-product of a powerful position. Urgency is a reaction to threat, danger, and fear. The perceived likelihood and seriousness of negative consequences are factors that determine urgency. AT&T used to be a monolithic giant with no reason to think about change. Divestiture forced the organization to split and the company was no longer operating in a monopolistic environment. This change created a sense of urgency among all AT&T employees as the company found itself competing for business. AT&T has fared well in the marketplace because it was able to embrace the need for change and implement one of the most effective change efforts ever. AT&T has won three Baldrige Awards and is one of two American companies to ever win a Deming prize.

If you aren't facing a real crisis that creates a sense of urgency, the right data can help create a sense of urgency. Finding out what your customers really think about your products and services might provide the data needed to create a sense of urgency. According to Harvard Business School professor John Kotter, a sense of urgency is strong enough when 75 percent of the company's management is convinced that business-as-usual will not be acceptable in the future. For further information on how to create a sense of urgency in your organization, refer to *The New Rules: How to Succeed in Today's Post Corporate World* by John Kotter.

Engage an Outside Agency or Consultant to Help Evaluate Your Progress and Develop an Action Plan

One reason that change programs fail is that companies believe they've already become world class after just a few years of effort. In other words, they declare victory before they've really won the war. They rely on their own employees, who are leading the change effort, to tell senior management how much progress they've made. The only way to know for sure how much progress has been made is to employ an objective third party to conduct an assessment and establish a baseline against which to measure progress.

An inexpensive approach to getting a good outside assessment is to prepare an application for one of the state-level quality awards that are based on the Baldrige. For an application fee of one to two thousand dollars (that is the general range), you will receive feedback from a team of six or more individuals from other organizations who have been trained in the Baldrige criteria. The assessment identifies your strengths and weaknesses and points out opportunities for improvement. TRW's ESL Division in Sunnyvale, California, applied for the California Quality Award just to get the feedback. The company ended up winning an award along with receiving the detailed performance assessment that it was looking for.

After an outside source evaluates your organization, you may want to hire a consultant to help develop an improvement plan. The key to successful action plans is to concentrate on a few key projects rather than to try to address all of the areas that need improvement.

A number of organizations have good results the first few years of their change effort. Major processes improve and dramatic results appear on initial projects. Morale is high during the first years and everyone is convinced that the program is going to be around for a long time and will revolutionize the organization. In the third or fourth year of the change initiative, the results become more difficult to attain. In addition, later results are not nearly as dramatic as those achieved during the first couple of years. Employees begin to lose interest and wonder whether the change effort will last or if it is on the way out.

Organizations that use the Baldrige criteria to evaluate their progress toward becoming world class typically plateau when they achieve 400 points out of the possible 1000. An organization can earn 400 points easily, but to attain 600 or 700 points it must make major investments and changes in the organizational culture and operations. Consequently, most companies plateau at the 400-point level and, if they are not careful, can begin to lose some of the ground gained earlier in the change effort. Here are a few approaches to use if your organization appears to have stalled in its effort to change.

Progress and results have plateaued

- Set a stretch goal and reengineer outdated processes and systems.
- Establish positive consequences for achieving stretch goals.

Set a Stretch Goal and Reengineer Outdated Processes and Systems

If your organization is stuck and the pace at which improvements are completed has dropped off dramatically, something needs to be done to rekindle enthusiasm, build momentum, and remove the barriers that prevent the organization from getting to the next level in your journey to becoming world class. One way to get employees excited again is to establish a meaningful goal, such as winning an award, attaining certified status for a key customer (e.g., Ford's Q-1), or getting some other form of recognition on a local or national level. The goal of Corning's CEO Jamie Houghton was to list his company among *Fortune* magazine's most admired companies. For a smaller company, a stretch goal might be a mention on *INC* magazine's annual list of the fastest growing small companies. Whatever award or recognition you decide to strive for, make certain that it is realistic and attainable. Do not prime the organization for failure.

A small company set a goal to achieve a California Quality Award in 1994, become a finalist for Baldrige in 1995, and win a Baldrige Award in 1996. Setting an appropriate stretch goal to motivate employees is only half of the battle. The hard part is to remove the barriers that are preventing you from reaching your goal. The barriers are often things such as your organizational structure or compensation system—things that are ingrained in the organization. For example, the need to change the compensation system may arise as you are making changes in job structure and responsibility to accommodate redesigned processes. This is where the need to reengineer outdated processes comes in. You often have to make major changes to systems that you are reluctant to change, but these are the changes that you need to regain momentum and progress to the next level.

Establish Positive Consequences for Achieving Stretch Goals

Winning a Baldrige Award or getting your company listed in *Fortune* may be exciting to executives, but it's rarely as thrilling to all employees. A good way to motivate employees to work toward stretch goals is to establish an internal award or recognition program. Cargill, a $50,000,000,000 agricultural company, motivates its employees to improve business unit performance through its annual award, which is based on the Baldrige criteria. Employees from winning organizations are invited to attend a three-day conference and awards ceremony in Minneapolis each year. This is actually quite rewarding to employees who may not travel for business and who are located all over the world.

Westinghouse has a similar internal awards program. Along with the trophy, Westinghouse used to give the winning business unit $200,000 to use in whatever fashion it wanted. Some distributed the money to employees as bonuses; others built a health club or day care facility. Westinghouse was recently forced to discontinue this practice when company profits and stock performance failed to reach desired levels. Whatever you do to reward employees for reaching stretch goals, make sure that the winners will really consider the prize a reward. Attending a stuffy company dinner and receiving a $25 bonus check may not be perceived as a reward by all employees. The key to making employee-recognition programs work is to tailor them to your culture and your employees. For further information on positive reinforcement in the work setting, read *Bringing out the Best in People* by Aubrey Daniels or *1001 Ways to Reward Employees* by Bob Nelson.

5. The Change Program Is Not Embraced Because It Was Forced on the Organization

Today, most large companies are putting a great deal of pressure on their suppliers to have systems in place to ensure consistently high-quality products and services. If you sell to European customers, chances are they require ISO 9000 certification before they will consider doing business with your firm. North American companies are feeling similar pressure from their key customers. Motorola requires all of its suppliers to submit an application for the Malcolm Baldrige Award. The American automakers have a new set of standards, taken from ISO 9000, that all of their suppliers must meet by 1997. Corporations are reducing the number of suppliers they buy from, and those that remain need to demonstrate that they have systems in place to ensure good quality products and services. Some companies have even developed their own programs to certify their suppliers, and certification is mandatory for a continued relationship.

Some organizations grudgingly comply with key customers' requirements by doing the minimum to keep the customer happy. Many will change their systems/processes enough so that it appears that they are undertaking a TQM effort (or whatever approach the customer is demanding) without really changing anything of substance. Others refuse to comply, assuming that it will cost them so much time and money to meet the requirements that they can no longer be competitive. A few others take a different approach. They do not see the mandate as a threat from the customer but rather as an opportunity to get support for improving their operations. These are the organizations that end up getting long-term business from their key customers and find that their improvement efforts for one customer help them improve their results for all customers. Here are a few approaches to use if key customers are forcing your organization to implement change.

The change program is not embraced because it was forced on the organization

- Educate senior management on the benefits of being a customer-focused organization.

- Enlist your customers to help design and implement your change effort.

- Negotiate shorter-term progress goals.

Educate Senior Management on the Benefits of Being a Customer-Focused Organization

  Implementing a change effort because it has become a criteria for continued business with major companies is certainly not an ideal situation to find yourself in. Some organizations, however, have used this situation as an opportunity to make a real impact on the way their companies do business. The suggestion from a key customer that you need to implement a TQM effort or other type of change program will get the attention of senior management quickly. That is the time to convince senior management that the proposed changes offer the opportunity to improve your organization and that it can reap the benefits from change not only with this customer, but the rest of your customer base as well.

The key to creating a positive situation is to show upper management the distinct benefits to doing more than the minimum to satisfy a particular customer. You need to sell senior management on the idea that something worth doing is worth doing right. A number of organizations have found that change efforts such as TQM have had handsome bottom-line payoffs. Solectron, a San Jose circuit board manufacturer, won a Baldrige Award in 1992, and its stock price has increased 1400 percent over a five-year period! It was one of the top five performing companies in *Forbes* 1995 summary of the performance of approximately 1,200 publicly traded companies. Evidence that being a customer-focused organization pays off is hard to ignore. Winners of the Baldrige Award, as a group, perform more than three times better in the stock market than the S&P 500. Gather hard evidence of the benefits of change, arrange site visits to companies that have been through the change, and get your executives talking to the executive staff from the customer organization to convince your team that it needs to embrace the change and reap the benefits from a fully implemented program.

Enlist Your Customers to Help Design and Implement Your Change Efforts

 If customers are mandating a prescribed change effort, ask them for their assistance. Most will be surprisingly helpful. Remember, it is in their best interest for you to become more customer focused, so they will probably do much more to help you than you might expect. Appleton Papers, the company that invented carbonless paper, holds regular tours and education sessions for its customers and suppliers to teach them how to use TQM to improve their businesses. Appleton, a finalist for the 1994 Baldrige Award, hosts over 100 companies a year in its training programs and tours. Appleton expends a great amount of time, effort, and money helping its customers and suppliers improve their performance using TQM.

Most corporations known to have a customer-focused culture will allow suppliers to attend their training programs free of charge. Some will even provide free consulting assistance. Most suppliers don't take advantage of the opportunity for training and consulting because they don't have the interest or, worse yet, because they are afraid of letting the customer see their weaknesses. These companies are missing a prime opportunity to cement a positive relationship with customers by enlisting their aid. Not only will you learn from your customers but you are also likely improve your standing with them by showing a willingness to learn, to listen to suggestions for improvement, and to implement positive changes in your organization. For related information, see "Offer Joint Training Sessions" in Chapter 15.

Negotiate Shorter-Term Progress Goals

Major companies realize that they can call the shots with their suppliers and have gotten to the point where they are tired of asking for voluntary compliance. They have tried many forms of assistance to help suppliers improve their processes and products/services, but many have declined. Consequently, the organizations have established strict qualification standards for their vendors and suppliers that often go beyond product or service quality and actually determine how suppliers manage their own organizations.

If your company has waited too long to implement an improvement effort and is now being pressured by your customers, you need an interim solution to relieve the pressure so that you can plan a long-term effort. An approach that has worked is to negotiate shorter-term progress goals with your customer. For example, if your customer is demanding that you become ISO 9000 certified within two years and you do not believe that you can accomplish that, see if you can show evidence of progress to satisfy the customer's annual goals

and renegotiate the date by which certification is required. One small parts manufacturer for the telecommunications industry satisfied its customer by setting the following annual progress goals:

Year One   Identify and document all key production/distribution processes.

Year Two   Develop process measures and standards and begin data collection on all key measures.

Year Three   Eliminate 75 percent of current inspectors while showing continuous improvement in levels of product quality.

Most customers are interested in evidence of continuous improvement on the part of their suppliers. In most cases any deadline is negotiable, as long as there is a good faith effort on your organization's part to comply. The customer may need you as much as you need it, so the customer's best interest is served by helping you succeed. Do not panic when you receive a deadline that you believe your organization cannot possibly meet. Talk to your customer and renegotiate in good faith. The most common cause of failure (and the worst thing you can do) is to try to change too much over a short period of time. Successful change and improvement comes gradually.

PART III

STRUCTURE AND SYSTEMS

In Part I, we discussed illnesses with strategy and leadership. In Part II, we explored implementation disorders. Now, in Part III, we must make sure that organizational systems and structures are healthy. Without the proper structure and systems in place, even the best qualified, most talented people can fail. If systems do not allow us to succeed, we cannot. The structure of the organization must support progress rather than impede it. Too often, though, bureaucratic organizations, where it takes a mountain of paperwork or political know-how to get things accomplished, are the norm. Common illnesses in the organization stem from structures that impede progress rather than promote it, from the lack of proper feedback mechanisms, from not having the right systems in place to measure the health of the organization, and from reinforcing or rewarding the wrong things. Read further to discover actions that can be taken to cure the common illnesses that can inhibit the health and viability of your organization.

Measures	Our measures don't give us a complete picture of the health of our organization.	Chapter 8
Structure	Our structure makes it hard to get things done.	Chapter 9
Feedback	We don't always know how well we are doing.	Chapter 10
Rewards	We reinforce and reward the wrong things.	Chapter 11

8 Measures

Our measures don't give us a complete picture of the health of our organization.

What you choose to measure indicates what you believe is important to the success strategy for the organization. Once something is measured and tracked, it gets the attention of management and employees alike as they work to improve performance in that area. Thus, selecting the wrong measures can cause failure because the organization focuses its efforts in the wrong place. It would be much like monitoring only the blood pressure of the patient who is in danger of developing heart problems because of elevated cholesterol levels. The patient might suffer a massive heart attack before doctors realize that they are monitoring the wrong vital sign. The intent was to prevent a heart attack, but because the wrong indicators were monitored, it happened anyway.

Organizations tend to focus on financial results to the exclusion of measures such as customer satisfaction, quality, and employee morale. Focusing exclusively on short-term financial results can cause an organization to mortgage its future. Strategies such as downsizing, slashing R&D expenditures, and consolidating locations make profits look better only in the short run. The loss to the organization over the long run can be devastating as talent is lost, product innovation slows down, and facilities are crowded and lack any room for growth. Although many organizations have started to turn their focus from the financial measures to the quality and customer satisfaction related measures, most still have a long way to go. If you believe your difficulties are caused by the lack of appropriate measurement systems, begin your search by reviewing the symptoms listed in the chart that follows and identifying the most likely cause of your difficulties.

Symptoms

The president or CEO regularly reviews performance on an overwhelming number of measures. (1)

Managers and technical professionals don't read a majority of the reports that they get. (1)

There is a lot of data, but little information. People cannot tell you what the real levels of performance have been. (1, 2)

There appears to be little connection between our vision and what we measure. (2, 3)

Each unit/location measures performance differently. (1, 2, 3)

Causes

1. Too many measures make it difficult to track progress.

2. Measures focus primarily on short-term financial or operational performance.

3. Measurable goals and objectives were established arbitrarily.

Now turn to the cause that seems to be the most likely source of your problem.

1. Too many measures make it difficult to track progress

Imagine trying to drive your car if you had to continually monitor a dash board with more than 50 gauges and indicator lights. You would be distracted from watching the road and would eventually cause an accident or run your car off the road. Many organizations today are being distracted from their work by trying to measure too many things. One aerospace company spent a year reengineering its measurement system to narrow down the measures to what it considered the "vital few." The company was able to reduce several hundred different indexes to 64 key results measurements. In our opinion, 64 is hardly the vital few. That is still an extremely large number of variables to measure. In this section we'll review some actions that you can take to streamline your measurement system so that you can do a better job of focusing on a few key factors that will guarantee long-term success and survival.

> Too many measures make it difficult to track progress

- Develop criteria for screening out extraneous data.
- Track no more than 15 to 20 key performance measures.

Chapter 8   **Measures**

Develop Criteria for Screening Out Extraneous Data

One of the first steps in simplifying your measurement system is to develop a tight set of criteria for selecting the best measures. A good set of criteria should be narrow enough to screen out extraneous measures. Some companies have used criteria such as "important," "objectively measurable," and "linked to the organization's success." Criteria like these are too general; you could make a case for including just about anything in your measurement system. FMC Corporation's Lithium Division has an excellent measurement system that is tied directly to its long-term vision and key success factors. It has 16 key measures, with 4 in each of the following categories:

- Financial performance

- Customer satisfaction

- Innovation/growth

- Internal performance

FMC developed a set of criteria that were used to select the 16 key performance measures. To be included in the overall performance measures, each index had to

- Be linked directly to one or more key business drivers.

- Fit into one of the four categories of data outlined above.

- Be an index of overall division performance.

- Be able to be tracked and reported at least once a month.

- Allow for specific improvement objectives to be set.

- Be able to be cascaded down to the different levels and facilities in the division.

- Have all executives agree on the inclusion of the index in the data base.

The criteria allowed FMC to focus on what it needed to measure in order to gauge organizational performance rather than to use whatever data were available. For more information on developing specific criteria and measures, consult *Vital Signs* by Steve Hronec.

Track No More Than 15 to 20 Key Performance Measures

Although we recommend that you have no more than 20 overall corporate measures, some organizations have narrowed down their measures to only a few key ones. Organizations like AT&T concentrate on three key performance measures that are all related to building the value of the corporation. Measures include

- Economic value added (financial performance).

- Customer value added (customer satisfaction and competitive pricing).

- People value added (employee satisfaction).

When you actually start to pare down the number of measures you track, you will most likely have a difficult time limiting them to 20—especially when you consider that your corporate scorecard needs to include measures of

- Financial performance.

- Customer satisfaction.

- Employee satisfaction.
- Product/service quality.
- Environmental and safety.
- Supplier performance.
- Operational performance (e.g., productivity, cycle time).

Most organizations collect and report on at least 15 to 20 financial measures alone, so it is easy to see why the number of measures that organizations track grows quickly. The key to keeping the total number of measures to a manageable number is to develop indexes that are a composite of a number of individual performance measures. For example, IBM measures what it calls the net satisfaction index (NSI), which is an overall measure of customer satisfaction. The NSI is based upon data collected for the following measures:
- Market share.
- Repeat/lost customers.
- Revenue from existing customers.
- Complaints.
- Telephone survey.
- Mail/fax survey.
- Customer focus group data.

Another company has an aggregate statistic called the employee satisfaction index (ESI). The ESI is made up of the following individual measures:
- Biannual climate survey.
- Absenteeism.
- Employee focus-group data.
- Voluntary turnover and transfers.
- Stress index.

The stress index is the most interesting. It is computed by tracking stress-related illnesses of employees, the average number of hours worked per week by both salaried and hourly employees, and the average number of hours spent traveling for business each week.

For additional reading, consult *Keeping Score: Using the Right Metrics to Drive World-Class Performance* by Mark Graham Brown.

℞ 2. Measures Focus Primarily on Short-Term Financial and Operational Performance

In many companies, you are only as good as last quarter's financial results. These companies collect data on a number of nonfinancial and longer term measures, but those are not the reports that get scrutinized and discussed in senior management meetings. By focusing their attention on meeting short-term revenue and profit goals, organizations mortgage their future. Financial performance is always important, but so are longer-term measures such as new product development, employee morale, and customer satisfaction. In this section we will examine some actions you can take to round out your corporate measurement system and ensure that you have a balanced focus on both long- and short-term performance.

Measures focus primarily on short-term financial and operational performance

- Develop measures that encourage innovation and new product/service development.
- Design systems for tracking customer-satisfaction levels.
- Design systems for measuring employee satisfaction or job fulfillment.
- Derive measures from key success factors or key business drivers.

Develop Measures That Encourage Innovation and New Product/Service Development

One way for any organization to ensure that it will remain ahead of the competition is to place importance on research and development (R&D) of new and innovative products and services. Developing the right measures to make certain the organization is properly focused is tricky. One R&D facility kept track of the number of patents its researchers received, the numbers of articles they published in professional journals, and the number of presentations they made at major conferences. Lots of useless devices got patented and plenty of research that had no marketable application was published. The facility got what it measured.

Innovation, growth, and product development are critical to the future of any company, but you need measures that drive the right performance. Air Products and Chemicals is a $3,000,000,000 company whose future depends on continually developing and marketing new products. It competes with several world-class companies like Dupont and Baldrige winner Eastman Chemicals. One of the measures Air Products has in its corporate scorecard is the percentage of sales derived each year from new products. The company sets more challenging goals on an annual basis as new products are the key to the company's continued growth. The measure of new product sales is an index of both R&D and marketing/sales.

Other R&D measures might include
• Percentage of sales derived from upgraded products.

• Average number of new products released annually.

• Overall percentage of time spent on new product development versus product modifications or fixes.

Design Systems for Tracking Customer-Satisfaction Levels

Most organizations today measure customer satisfaction. However, in most cases, they collect far too little data on this important index of company performance. The typical approach is to mail out a survey once a year and hope that customers take the time to complete it and send it back. Another common way to measure customer satisfaction is to track customer complaints.

To be really useful, your customer satisfaction measurement system should contain two types of data:
• Hard measures of customer buying behavior (market share, repeat business, etc.).

• Soft measures of customer opinion (surveys, complaints, focus groups, etc.).

Collecting data on customer opinion or attitude is important because these data help you identify potential or real problems and correct them before they result in lost business. The keys to getting the information you need are to select the right method and to ask the right people the right questions. For example, don't ask the company's executives how they feel your response-time-to-order has been over the past year. Ask those questions of the people who do the product ordering or of those who receive and use the materials. The method you select will have to be a trade-off among time, dollars, and the response rate targeted, and it will be dependent on your relationship with the customer. The following chart gives you an overview of the strengths and weaknesses of three primary data-collection methods.

	Face-to-Face or Focus Group Interview	Telephone Survey	Mail Survey
Flexibility in data collection	S	M	W
Quantity of data obtainable	S	M	W
Speed of data collection	M	S	W
Geographic coverage	W	S	S
Identity of respondents	S	M	W
Sample results representative of the population	W	S	M
Reduced investigator bias	W	M	S
Reduced nonresponse bias	S	M	W

S = strong   M = medium   W = weak

It's important to keep in mind that customers are busy and often do not have a significant amount of time to spend giving you feedback on your performance.

Hard measures of customer behavior are much more revealing. Many people are uncomfortable complaining or putting negative comments on a survey, especially when the responses are identifiable. All organizations need to have good data on the number of customers gained and lost and other measures of customer buying-behavior. Behavior is the true indi-

cator of how people feel. For additional information, consult *The Customer Driven Company* by Richard Whitely, *Managing Customer Value* by Bradley Gale, or *Measuring Customer Satisfaction* by Richard Gerson.

Design Systems for Tracking Employee Satisfaction or Job Fulfillment

 Employee satisfaction is a prerequisite to customer satisfaction. Employees who are unhappy with their jobs, bosses, and working conditions will never give a significant amount of extra effort to their work. Companies that have focused on delighting their employees, such as AT&T Universal Card, have found that employee satisfaction really can lead to high levels of profit and customer satisfaction. To do this, your organization needs to have a good way of measuring employee well-being and morale. Your measurement of employee satisfaction should include hard measures, (e.g., turnover and absenteeism) and soft measures (e.g., work climate surveys).

If you do nothing else, you should at least conduct an employee survey once each year to find out how employees feel about their jobs, the work environment, and the organization. We recommend using an outside firm to conduct the survey for several reasons. First of all, employees will be much more likely to be honest if they send the surveys to an outside firm. In addition, outside companies will be able to tell you how your results compare to those of similar companies and perhaps give you an industry rating to which you can compare your performance. The danger of an employee satisfaction survey is that you establish the expectation in the employee's minds that things will change for the better. Your employees will assume that you are asking where the problems are because you want to fix them. If your organization is likely to ignore or rationalize negative results rather than deal with them, don't even bother with the survey. You will simply create more frustration in the organization.

For a good book that explains AT&T's approach to delighting their employees and using employee satisfaction measures to drive the business, see *Incredibly American* by Marilyn Zuckerman and Lewis Hatala.

Derive Measures from Key Success Factors or Business Drivers

The key to a sound business strategy is to do something others cannot do or do something well that others have difficulty doing. Once you have developed a sound business strategy, you need to identify key success factors that will allow you to remain ahead of your competition and/or to be successful in today's economic environment. Key success factors might include competitive pricing, higher quality, or better service. Developing a good strategy and identifying the key success factors or business drivers needed for your long-term success is the foundation upon which to build good performance measurement systems. There have been instances where organizations have done a good job of defining key success fac-

tors, but have failed to link these success factors to their measurement systems. For example, one organization identified being the lowest cost supplier in the market as a key success factor for its long-term growth; the company scorecard did not include any measures associated with competitive pricing. This organization would have difficulty determining whether it truly was the lowest cost supplier.

Other companies do a fairly good job of linking their measures and key business drivers. One aerospace company decided that a key success factor was to decrease its reliance on government contracts, since defense budgets are predicted to continue shrinking. Two key measures that are tracked and reviewed by the CEO each month are (1) total value of outstanding proposals for nongovernment work and (2) monthly sales revenues derived from nongovernmental work. For further information on linking measures and key success factors, consult *Vital Signs* by Steve Hronec.

A measure without a goal is meaningless information. For example, stepping on a scale each day is of no use if you've never determined a goal weight. A goal tells us what we are trying to achieve or specifies the acceptable level of performance. Goals must be set carefully. Should they be set too high, employees become discouraged and stop trying; if they are set too low, employees achieve the goal in the first quarter and coast for the rest of the year. Employees in most companies have learned the trick to goal setting: Set the goal high enough so that the boss thinks you will have to hustle but low enough to be achievable. The trick is finding that proper balance. In this section, we'll review a couple of actions that you can take to improve your goals or objectives.

Measurable goals and objectives were set arbitrarily

- Set goals based on competitors' and/or benchmark organizations' performance.

- Involve employees, suppliers, and/or customers in the goal-setting process.

Set Goals Based on Competitors' and/or Benchmark Organizations' Performance

Many otherwise well-run organizations have an approach to goal setting and planning that has been used since the 1960s. Management by objectives (MBO) refuses to die. Using MBO, goals and objectives are set by looking at how the organization performed last year and bumping up the results by 5 to 10 percent to establish next year's target. Some organizations have 10-percented themselves right out of business. Others have dropped the MBO approach in favor of "stretch goals." Stretch goals can be equally problematic as they too are often set in a completely arbitrary fashion. For example, one company established an overall company goal of "80 in 5," which meant that all performance measures needed to show an 80 percent improvement in five years. The problem was that the goals were simply made up because they sounded good.

Goals need to be based on research. Research should include a study of your biggest competitors, particularly those that do a better job than you, those that are gaining significant market share, or those that are making inroads to your customer base. Your research should also include a study of benchmark-level companies outside of your industry. This technique is particularly useful for setting goals for support areas like finance, procurement, or human resources. Benchmark companies can give your organization a realistic view of how quickly goals can be achieved and reset. Goals should be set only after conducting thorough research. Remember, goals should push the organization a little harder to achieve success, but not be so hard or unrealistic that they are not attainable. A good reference on using benchmarking to help set organizational goals and objectives is *Strategic Benchmarking* by Gregory Watson.

Involve Employees, Suppliers, and/or Customers in the Goal-Setting Process

An important approach to setting good goals is to get a lot of input from both internal and external sources. Some leading organizations involved their employees, key suppliers, and even customers in the goal-setting processes. These groups can perform a "reality check" on what executive management believes can and should be accomplished. Employees who work throughout the organization know the limits of each particular area and can give management guidance on what is realistic and how the area will be impacted by trying to meet the goal. Suppliers can give input on whether the goods or services they provide will perform well enough to allow the organization to meet its goals. When suppliers are aware of the goals that your organization is trying to achieve, they can work to modify their own products or processes to help you reach those goals. "Partnering" with suppliers to achieve organizational goals is very effective.

In addition, goals must be well linked to high-priority customer requirements. The organization needs to understand and link its goals to customer expectations, requirements, and desires. For example, an HMO set its goal for claims processing at 30 days without ever asking customers how long they expected to wait for a claim to be processed. If customers expect claims to be processed within two weeks, the HMO will have many irate customers.

Although involving suppliers, employees, and customers in the goal-setting process has been part of the Baldrige Award criteria since 1988, the practice is not common in most organizations today. For further information on ways to involve customers and suppliers in goal setting, see *Real-Time Strategic Change* by Robert Jacobs.

9 Structure

Our structure makes it hard to get things done.

The way an organization and jobs are structured can inhibit or facilitate progress. Traditionally, organizations have been structured around the birds-of-a-feather concept: put people who do the same job together. This often leads to fiefdoms and stove-pipe organizations where a decision must wend its way to the top of one functional area and back down another. This bureaucratic model worked relatively well during the industrial revolution, but in this age of turbulent change, it's an albatross. What's the antidote?

First, make sure you are not structured around an inefficient process. Mapping and improving the work process is often a good place to begin. A work process (such as developing new products or fulfilling customer orders) often crosses organizational boundaries, resulting in handoffs and delays. Many of our suggested actions focus on eliminating or mitigating this problem.

Looking at the technical aspects of work is only one part of the treatment, for people are involved and employees don't do their best work if the jobs are designed poorly or if their expertise becomes dated.

Review the following symptoms and choose a cause that seems to be the most likely culprit. Then turn to the section for that cause to identify a course of action.

Symptoms

It takes too long to make the product, serve the customer, or complete the task. (1, 2, 4)

Quality is not what it should be. (2, 3)

Rework and redundancy are killing our productivity. (1, 2)

It takes lots of meetings and sign-offs to get anything done. (1, 2, 4)

We're losing our edge and becoming dated. (5)

We don't know where to go to solve a problem. (2, 4)

Employees are bored and don't seem to care about their work. (6)

We find ourselves reinventing the wheel, and then discovering that someone else in the organization has already solved the problem or addressed the issue. (4)

Causes

1. Inefficient work processes.

2. Functional fiefdoms.

3. Employees don't understand how they affect downstream operations.

4. Incompatibilities across the organization make it difficult to communicate, learn, and coordinate.

5. Specialists'/experts' knowledge becoming outdated.

6. Poor job design leaves employees bored and without a sense of ownership.

1. Inefficient Work Processes

In many organizations, tracking a work process is as convoluted as an Agatha Christie mystery. All the players have incomplete knowledge, documents vanish behind closed doors never to be seen again, no one is quite sure who did what when, and separating out the relevant from the irrelevant becomes a major task.

Streamlining the work is often the best way to improve an organization's performance and employees' sanity. We recommend several common approaches that can be used individually or together to improve organizational performance.

Inefficient work processes

- Reengineer.

- Appoint a process owner.

- Implement a quality improvement team.

- Automate.

- Outsource the work.

- Spin out the venture.

- Create a self-directed team.

Reengineer

Reengineering represents a radical rethinking of how work is accomplished given the existing and emerging technologies. Many of our work processes have changed little since the precopier days of green eyeshades. Now with wireless and satellite communications, information superhighways, and such, many things that were impossible are now possible. Often, you can eliminate entire steps in a process, drastically improving performance. For example, many organizations are eliminating the need to send or receive invoices.

Reengineering involves questioning why everything is done, whether it needs to be done, and who should do it. Reengineering often includes automation, outsourcing, self-directed teams, and organizational restructuring around a process. Non-value-added steps and handoffs are minimized. For more information, see *Reengineering Work* by Hammer and Champy, or "Don't Automate: Obliterate" also by Michael Hammer. See also *Business Process Improvement: The Breakthrough Strategy for Total Quality, Productivity, and Competitiveness* by H. James Harrington.

Appoint a Process Owner

If you can't restructure around the process, you can assign an executive to "own" and oversee each process. First, define the major processes in the organization (e.g., order fulfillment, and new product development). Then assign an executive to each process who can instigate and implement improvements across organizational boundaries. Often a quality improvement team is established to recommend changes to each process. For more information, see *Improving Organizational Performance: How to Manage the White Space on the Organization Chart* by Rummler and Brache, and "Forget Functions, Manage Processes" by Robert Blaha.

Implement a Quality Improvement Team

Quality improvement teams are temporary task forces, usually of front-line employees, that are charged with recommending improvements to a work process. These teams can be used without the cumbersome structures commonly known as quality circles. Total quality tools (such as brainstorming, Pareto charts, affinity diagrams, and statistical process control charts) help these teams analyze problems and identify solutions. For more information, see *The Team Handbook* by Peter Scholtes. For information on the quality tools, see *The Memory Jogger Plus* by Michael Brassard.

Automate

Sometimes human work can be performed better by machines or computers. Good candidates for automation include tasks that are tedious, dangerous, or fraught with human error. Talk to engineers, vendors, and others in your industry for ideas about how to use automation to improve performance. One caution: Don't just automate an inefficient process; rethink how the task should be performed given the new technology. For interesting insights on using information technologies to improve your future competitiveness, see *The Virtual Corporation* by Davidow and Malone.

Outsource the Work

 Every organization has things it's good at and things it's not. More and more, organizations are outsourcing many of their noncore tasks. Print shops, mail rooms, cafeterias, training, transportation, and other departments are rapidly being populated by employees of contract firms. Ask yourself, what value added, what distinctive competence do we bring? If your answer is that others can do this task better, contract with them to provide the service. See "Innovators in Outsourcing" by Howard Anderson, *When Giants Learn to Dance* by Rosabeth Moss Kanter, and *Liberation Management* by Tom Peters. One warning, however: Be careful not to outsource something that will be crucial to your success in the future.

Spin Off the Venture

   This option is similar to outsourcing. The difference is that instead of contracting with an outside firm, thus displacing employees, the organization "spins off" its existing department so it becomes its own company. Sometimes the organization remains a subsidiary of the parent company, or it can be divested all together. While this option is often disruptive, it does reenergize the entrepreneurial spirit and creativity. See *Intrapreneuring* by Gifford Pinchot III. Also see "What Will We Find in an Intrapreneur's Rabbit Hole" by Darcy Hitchcock.

ABB Asea Brown Boveri is a $30,000,000,000 electrical engineering firm that has received a great deal of attention. ABB has created a global matrix of over 1,300 separate operating companies, which has allowed the company to resolve the paradoxes of the 21st century, "to be simultaneously global and local, big and small, centralized and decentralized." See "Changing the Role of Top Management: Beyond Structure to Processes" by Ghoshal and Bartlett.

Create a Self-Directed Team

   Many of the options above primarily create a one-time improvement. For example, you reengineer a process that works well until the technology or customer needs change again. A different approach is to create a team populated by all those involved in a process and empower them to improve the process. When the team is held jointly accountable for outcomes and is linked directly to customers, the results often lead to continuous improvement. One of our clients who implemented these teams reduced its cycle time from five weeks to five days. For more information on self-directed teams, see *The Wisdom of Teams* by Katzenbach and Smith, and *Why Teams Can Fail and What to Do about It* by Hitchcock and Willard. See also "Participative Design Works, Partially Participative Doesn't" by Steven Cabana.

2. Functional Fiefdoms

Traditionally, organizations have been structured functionally, putting those of like functions together: accounting, engineering, operations, maintenance. This structure is easy to manage since all the individuals in a department do similar work. The problem is that this structure creates bureaucracies and fiefdoms. To make improvements, you often must go up one chain of command and down another, dealing with people who often have more affinity for their profession than the organization.

In today's competitive climate, few organizations can afford this inefficiency. You basically have two choices: reward people for working together, across the organizational boundaries; or tear down the walls, putting interdependent people together. In our view, the latter structure is usually preferable.

Functional fiefdoms

- Reorganize around a whole piece of work.
- Compensate people based on group outcomes.
- Create cross-functional teams.

Reorganize around a Whole Piece of Work

In a typical functional organization, the people who work together are not interdependent. They work side-by-side, not together. Those who need their results or who must provide them with input are in different departments. This solution destroys the functional structure and reorganizes the business around a complete piece of work. Although organizing around a work process has become fashionable, you should consider many options. These options include organizing by

- Customer or customer group—If your customers or markets have distinctly different needs you can often serve them better by establishing teams that are dedicated to their needs. A construction firm may denote separate teams or divisions to building schools, hospitals, and high rises.

- Product or service—If each product or service requires specialized knowledge or equipment, this organizational structure may work well. However, you may need a "front office" organized by customer to act as a liaison to the product or service teams.

- Project—Increasingly, all work is becoming project work, with each project requiring a different mix of skills and knowledge. Teams form and reform around each project, and individuals may work on several teams simultaneously. It is chaotic to manage but provides the greatest flexibility. See *Liberation Management* by Tom Peters.

- Geography—Where geographic differences are significant or distribution of resources is difficult, organizing by geography makes sense. The obvious application is in international businesses (you may not be fluent in Greek *and*

Thai). However, janitorial and maintenance services may be organized by building, and hospital staff may be organized into teams that serve one wing of a hospital.

See "Participative Design Works, Partially Participative Doesn't" by Steven Cabana, and the *Work Redesign Team Handbook* by Darcy Hitchcock.

Compensate People Based on Group Outcomes

Where it is not possible to reorganize, the next best option is to make sure people are rewarded for working together. Some Fortune 100 companies have made a portion of an executive's bonus contingent upon the performance of other divisions. You can also offer gainsharing or profit sharing to employees. For this option to work, however, the individuals must feel they have influence over the performance of the larger organization. Therefore, employee involvement efforts are critical to gainsharing programs, and cross semination of executive ideas is important to making the executive bonus program work. See Chapter 11 for more on the topic of reinforcement. See also "Changing the Role of Top Management: Beyond Structure to Processes" by Ghoshal and Bartlett.

Create Cross-Functional Teams

Cross-functional teams that are assembled to solve organizational problems may also be a way to break down functional fiefdoms. In these settings, people come to understand each other's point of view. Cross-functional teams should have a clear charter. One approach is to implement a quality improvement team that is responsible for solving a cross-functional quality problem. Quality improvement teams are temporary task forces, usually of front-line employees, that are charged with recommending improvements to a work process. These can be used without the cumbersome structures commonly known as quality circles. Total quality tools (such as brainstorming, Pareto charts, affinity diagrams, and statistical process-control charts, etc.) help these teams analyze problems and identify solutions. For more information, see *The Team Handbook* by Peter Scholtes. For information on the quality tools, see *The Memory Jogger Plus* by Michael Brassard.

Similarly, you can assemble a task force to improve processes. This is often done by appointing an executive as "process owner." First, define the major processes in the organization (e.g., order fulfillment and new product development). Then assign an executive to each process who can instigate and implement improvements across organizational boundaries. Often a quality improvement team is established to recommend changes to each process. For more information, see *Improving Organizational Performance: How to Manage the White Space on the Organization Chart* by Rummler and Brache, and "Forget Functions, Manage Processes" by Robert Blaha.

3. Employees Don't Understand How They Affect Downstream Operations

An axiom in business is that you can't add quality back into a process. In other words, if something goes wrong early in the process, things can only get worse. If an order is taken incorrectly, for example, the customer is unlikely to get what he or she wanted, regardless of how well the order is filled. Often, employees have no idea how their error or omission affects others down the line.

In one manufacturing organization, a self-directed team decided to quit work at 10 AM on Friday. It had been working overtime on a special project and felt drained. From the team's perspective, the best thing the members could do was to go home and rest. What the workers didn't know—until the following Monday—was that they had shut down the whole plant. Oops!

Here are a few options for helping people understand how their job affects others.

> **Employees don't understand how they affect downstream operations**

- Cross train.
- Offer job rotation.
- Change physical layout.
- Trade jobs for a day.

Cross Train

The best way to help people understand the work of other employees is to train everyone thoroughly in all the tasks. This technique affords enormous flexibility, as employees can fill in for each other during vacations and help relieve bottlenecks. Since cross training is time-consuming, it should only be done when (1) you need the flexibility in staffing, (2) the employees will have regular opportunity to use the skills, and (3) the tasks require a moderate amount of training to learn.

If you choose this option, be systematic about the training. Don't let the training occur haphazardly. See Chapter 14 for more information on knowledge and skills.

Offer Job Rotation

Job rotation is a variation on cross training. Instead of cross training an individual in all of the steps of a process, an individual moves progressively from one position to another. The potential drawback of job rotation is that it can take a long time for people to learn all of the steps. However, when the tasks are quite complex and require significant training to perform, job rotation may be a better option than cross training.

Change Physical Layout

Sometimes just moving workers into closer proximity can cause more communication and understanding. Physical layout is an important factor in organizational performance. Facilitate communication by removing physical barriers so people can see one another and by providing convenient settings for employees to gather and share ideas. For example, a 3M building in Austin, Texas, was specifically designed to force interactions. "People are 'designed in' closer together. Functions are jumbled to cause chance connections. Blackboards and couches and coffee machines are placed next to bathrooms (creating so-called 'interactive nodes') to up the odds of productive interchange."[1]

Trade Jobs for a Day

In some cases trading jobs for a short period of time may be possible. You can find many examples of this practice in some model organizations. At Johnsonville Foods, for instance, each employee spends one day each year with an employee from another department. Honda managers are required to exchange jobs with another manager from a different department for a two-week period.[2]

---

1. T. Peters, *Liberation Management* (New York: Alfred A. Knopf, 1992), pp. 379–380.
2. N. Dixon, "A Practical Model for Organizational Learning," *Issues & Observations* 15, no. 2 (1995), pp. 1–4.

4. Incompatibilities across the Organization Make It Difficult to Communicate, Learn, and Coordinate

Sometimes organizations become so decentralized that they cannot take advantage of the potential synergies. For example, people often may not learn about needs, innovations, or solutions created in other parts of the organization. Here are a few options to consider.

Incompatibilities across the organization make it difficult to communicate, learn, and coordinate

- Centralize information functions.

- Develop linking structures.

- Hold an innovation-sharing or quality day.

- Establish goals and incentives to encourage sharing and discourage competition.

Centralize Information Functions

Information and knowledge—not cheap labor or raw materials—are going to be the critical organizational resources for much of the 21st century. To maximize performance, the information systems probably should be centralized (or linked), even when the rest of the organization is decentralized. Identify the critical information you need to gain the competitive edge and then design real-time information systems to meet those needs. With satellites, faxes, the Internet, and cellular phones, sharing critical information can be easier than ever.

Kao Corporation, for example, has created a sophisticated value-added network called Kao VAN. This information system empowered front-line employees to examine customer needs, design new products, and research latent technologies within the organization. In just seven years, Kao became Japan's number two cosmetics company, expanding beyond its historical base of soaps and detergent.[3] See "Changing the Role of Top Management: Beyond Structure to Processes" by Ghoshal and Bartlett. See also numerous articles in Forbes ASAP supplements.

Develop Linking Structures

In many cases, you won't need elaborate information systems. What you need are forums for people to come together to share information. Having linking structures such as team coordinators for cross-functional issues (e.g., training, quality, and information management) enables you to provide the infrastructure for these cross-functional meetings. Task forces, all-employee meetings, training sessions, and management retreats all present opportunities for serendipitous and structured sharing.

3M is a master at leveraging innovations across the corporation. For example, a nonwoven material developed in one division spawned many other products in 19 other divisions. This sharing is driven by 3M's cultural values and management practices. Products belong to divisions, but technology belongs to the company is one of their maxims.[4] For more on team-based organizations, see Ghoshal and Bartlett, and "Linking Arrangements and New Work Designs" by Kolodny and Dresner.

Hold an Innovation-Sharing or Quality Day

If you mostly want to improve innovation diffusion, often the best way is to have a day dedicated to sharing this information. Xerox, Monsanto, and others have held quality fairs where teams present their ideas and innovations. Work groups can design posters that explain their idea, or they can make formal presentations on their innovations.

---

3. Ghoshal and Bartlett, "Changing the Role of Top Management: Beyond Structure to Processes."

4. Ghoshal and Bartlett, "Changing the Role of Top Management: Beyond Structure to Processes."

Establish Goals and Incentives to Encourage Sharing and Discourage Competition

 Goals and incentives can be used to encourage cross-functional learning. For example, American Express had special awards, bonuses, and publicity for "One Enterprise" projects—and employees at any level of the organization were eligible. In addition, incentives called portfolio awards are determined not only by performance of individual business units but also by performance of all business units. Pillsbury appointed a synergy czar who used the title "Sr. vice president, blurring" on his business cards. Firestar created an interbusiness sector fund to pay for projects spanning organizational boundaries. For more information, see *When Giants Learn to Dance* by Rosabeth Moss Kanter, and "Changing the Role of Top Management" by Ghoshal and Bartlett.

5. Specialists'/Experts' Knowledge Becoming Outdated

Many organizations are responding to the problems of a functional structure by reorganizing entirely around a process. Specialists and staff positions are decentralized and assigned to each core work process. This organization has its own drawbacks, however.

Specialists gain an understanding and ownership of the core work of the organization but they lose the benefit of sharing ideas with professional colleagues. Often, their skills become outdated. They also lose the synergy and consistency they had in a functional structure.

Specialists'/experts' knowledge becoming outdated

- Create a matrix structure.
- Rotate through a staff function.

Create a Matrix Structure

One approach is to organize by process but link specialists through a matrixed structure. For example, the primary allegiance of an information systems (IS) staff member may be to the XYZ product line, but she or he may also be a member (via a dotted line) of the IS circle of excellence or "peer sphere." The staff member works full time on the product line but meets periodically with IS colleagues to discuss problems, work standards, and new technologies. This option earned a hard-to-do icon because managing priorities in a matrix organization can be difficult. Being beholden to more than one group can be confusing and cause conflicts. See the earlier section "Develop Linking Structures."

Rotate through a Staff Function

Another approach is to maintain a small staff department whose purpose is to conduct research and set organizational standards. Unlike traditional staff departments that often serve the purpose of cop, these staff departments serve as laboratories for new ideas. An individual rotates into the staff department for a short duration (often to complete a research project) and then returns to the lines to use his or her new knowledge.

Some of the most innovative drug companies have been using this strategy to speed innovations. They solve the problems of organizing by function and by process by mixing the pot, vacillating between the two extremes. For more information, see

"Managing Innovation in the Information Age" by Rebecca Henderson.

6. Poor Job Design Leaves Employees Bored and Without a Sense of Ownership

Job design is a major factor in employee satisfaction and performance. For employees to enjoy their work, their jobs must include these five factors:[5]

- Variety—A variety of tasks to perform.

- Importance—Tasks must seem important.

- Wholeness—Employees should complete a whole piece of work.

- Autonomy—Employees should have control over planning, scheduling, and evaluating the task.

- Feedback—Employees should receive performance feedback from the task itself.

---

5. Oldham and Hackman

Poor job design leaves employees bored and without a sense of ownership

- Provide for job enrichment/ enlargement.

- Provide cross training.

- Reorganize into teams.

- Link employees to customers.

Provide for Job Enrichment/Enlargement

One option is to increase the variety of tasks an individual performs. Look horizontally and vertically. To increase variety horizontally, you could add tasks before and after a particular step in a process. For example, an employee could learn how to operate more pieces of equipment that manufacture your product. To increase variety vertically, the employee could take on more of the "management" tasks such as planning the work (which affects autonomy as well). Vertical integration usually leads to self-directed teams where employees take on many of the responsibilities of a traditional supervisor. See *Productive Workplaces* by Marvin Weisbord for more information.

Provide Cross Training

Cross training is usually necessary when jobs are enlarged and employees take on new horizontal tasks. Since cross training can take a lot of time, it should only be done when (1) you need the flexibility in staffing, (2) the employees will have regular opportunities to use their skills, and (3) the tasks require a moderate amount of training to learn.

If you choose this option, be systematic about the training. Don't let the training occur haphazardly. See Chapter 14 for more information on knowledge and skills.

Reorganize into Teams

Work teams, such as self-directed or high-performance teams, incorporate all five of the job satisfaction factors. Workers form teams that complete a whole piece of work (wholeness and feedback); they manage themselves (autonomy and importance); and they often receive cross training (variety). For more information on self-directed teams, see *The Wisdom of Teams* by Katzenbach and Smith, and *Why Teams Can Fail and What to Do about It* by Hitchcock and Willard. For information about how to restructure into teams, see "Participative Design Works, Partially Participative Doesn't" by Steven Cabana, and *The Work Redesign Team Handbook: A Step-by-Step Guide to Creating Self-Directed Teams* by Darcy Hitchcock.

Link Employees to Customers

If feedback is the weakest link in the chain, linking employees directly with customers can be a powerful way to improve their performance. Suggestions include having them answer customer calls, visit a customer's site, conduct customer surveys, and review customer satisfaction data. Some organizations even find ways to include customers as members of their teams.

10 Feedback

We don't always know how well we are doing.

Feedback is the cornerstone of continuous improvement. Stepping on the scale regularly is what keeps us to our diets. Similarly, without current, relevant data about how well it is doing in its key business indicators, an organization will be ill-equipped to maintain a competitive edge. Getting the right information to the right people, however, isn't always as easy as it seems. Review the list of symptoms below to see if any match the difficulties your own organization may be having with closing the feedback loop.

Symptoms

People don't know how well they are doing. (1, 2)

The right information doesn't seem to get to the right people. (1)

People don't understand the feedback they get. (2, 3)

By the time we get the information, it's old news. (1)

People ignore the feedback they get. (2, 3)

We are uncomfortable giving feedback. (4, 5)

Causes

1. Employees don't get enough timely, relevant feedback.

2. Employees don't know how to interpret the data.

3. Employees don't know how to act on the data.

4. The people who give the feedback don't understand the job.

5. The feedback contributes to conflict and finger pointing.

1. Employees Don't Get Enough Timely, Relevant Feedback

Feedback is important to every person and every work unit in an organization. Unless it is given in a timely fashion and is specific to improvement needs, feedback will lose its impact. The strategies provided here will help you assure that the feedback your employees and departments get is focused, immediate, and complete.

Employees don't get enough timely relevant feedback

- Let front-line employees collect the data.
- Establish guidelines for collecting data.
- Report feedback in an actionable format.

Let Front-Line Employees Collect the Data

The best way to ensure that work units get the timely, relevant feedback they need is to give them responsibility for tracking and analyzing performance data themselves. This process begins with the identification of methods for measuring their own contribution to the organization's key measures. If the company is tracking waste, for example, the team should put in place its own measures for calculating waste within its own work unit. When the organizationwide data are reported, team members will have some basis for evaluating their own performance.

While five to six key measures are sufficient at the organizational level, the individual work units or teams need additional measures to track their internal work processes and group effectiveness. The work unit, like the organization, should be careful to measure what is important, not what is easy to measure. Teams should start with key questions related to their goals. For example, how quickly are we able to respond to our customers, what is the defect rate of the products we produce, or is this particular process value-added? Once the questions are identified, the team can then determine what data it needs to monitor its own performance.

For more information see Chapter 6 of *Why Teams Can Fail and What to Do about It* by Hitchcock and Willard.

Establish Guidelines for Collecting Data

Giving employees the responsibility for collecting their own data is the first step to assuring that they get useful feedback. If they have never done this task before, however, they may need some training on how to collect and analyze data. To be useful, feedback data must meet all the following criteria:

- Feedback must be immediate. The hallmark of the flexible organization is the ability to respond quickly to quality problems. This action is virtually impossible if you don't learn about your problems until well after the fact.

- Feedback must be reported often enough to reveal trends. Are we getting better? worse? stagnating?

- Feedback must also be valid. If the validity of the feedback is questionable, it will be difficult to draw credible conclusions. Consider these tips for assuring that the feedback you collect is valid:

  - Collect feedback data from a broad sample. Looking at only a few cases or interviewing only a couple of customers may not give you a complete picture.

  - Try to account for outside factors that could affect the data you collect (e.g., measuring delivery times during a trucking strike or conducting an employee satisfaction survey just after bonuses are distributed).

For more information on analyzing feedback see David Futrell's article "Ten Reasons Why Surveys Fail—Common Sampling and Measurement Errors."

Report Feedback in an Actionable Format

To be useful data must also be actionable. Data that are too broad don't provide enough information to solve problems. Learning that your customer satisfaction index is down is not helpful until you also learn what specifically caused the drop. This is as true for raw data as it is for verbal feedback. When designing measures, be careful to develop methods that provide actionable data. Asking customers to rate your service, for example, is an important but insufficient measure. It should be part of a survey process that asks for their feedback on a variety of specific performance measures (delivery time, availability of sales staff, clarity of documents, etc.).

Verbal feedback should be actionable as well. When soliciting verbal feedback make sure that it focuses on specific behaviors. It isn't helpful, for example, to hear that a team member is not "pulling his weight." It is more productive to pinpoint the specific practices (or their absence) that cause the problem (e.g., misses every other meeting, won't type his own reports, submits incomplete documents).

2. Employees Don't Know How to Interpret the Data

If you've ever had a doctor explain your condition in Latin medical terms, you know the frustration of receiving important yet incomprehensible feedback. Your employees may find themselves in a similar situation if they have to respond to feedback that they can't easily comprehend. It is critical to ensure that recipients of the feedback data can understand and interpret it. This important link is often missing in the organizational feedback loop and often results in piles of reports and charts that no one ever reads. If this is a problem in your organization, consider the following strategies.

Employees don't know how to interpret the data

- Provide training on statistics.
- Present data in graphic form.
- Focus feedback on specific performance.
- Ask for clarification.

Provide Training on Statistics

Some misinterpretation stems from a lack of familiarity with basic statistics and accounting practices. Interpreting even simple data will probably require an understanding of such statistical concepts as central tendency (average, median, mode), and variability (variance, standard deviation, range). Similarly, if employees are unfamiliar with accounting principles, they may need training on basic financial concepts such as depreciation, unit costing, or return on investment. Employees will also need to learn how to draw conclusions from data. One common error, for example, is assuming a cause and effect relationship from correlational data. This is the tendency to say that one thing causes another because the two always occur together—for example, concluding that equipment failure is caused by hot weather because the data indicate that equipment fails most often in July and August. Teams may need some training or consulting to help them interpret the data once the data have been collected and tabulated.

For more information see *Statistical Methods for Quality Improvement* by Alan Ryan.

Present Data in Graphic Form

Presentation format can strongly influence the ability to read and understand feedback data. Where possible, data should be presented in graphic form. This is especially true of numerical data; one picture is worth well more than a thousand words. Employees may still need training to help them read charts. Most people can understand basic pie, bar, and line charts. Run charts, Pareto diagrams, and complex matrices are very useful but less widely understood tools. The graphic format should also be well suited to the data. Pie charts, for example, are best suited for data that have a fixed maximum (percentages or distribution of dollars in a fixed budget). The intervals on charts must also be logical, clear, and comparable. You can, for example, make differences in variables look very large on a bar chart by making your intervals very small. A quick glance at a chart like that can give a false impression. Starting your graphs at something other than zero can have a similar effect.

Below is a summary of the most popular data presentation formats and their appropriate uses.

Histogram (bar chart)	Shows variations in a process.
Pareto chart (bar chart)	Organizes data in relative order.
Scatter diagram	Displays data to show what type of relationship, if any, exists between two variables.
Run chart	Displays information about a process taking place over time to show trends.
Gantt chart	Documents the schedule, events, and responsibilities for a particular project.
Fish bone diagram	Uses lines and words to show the relationship between an outcome and its causes.
Flow chart	Illustrates the sequence of steps or actions involved in a particular task.
Force field analysis	Displays the forces (both positive and negative) that influence your progress toward a goal.

For more information on these and other tools, see *The Quality Toolbox* by Nancy Tague, or William Cleveland's *The Elements of Graphing Data*.

Focus Feedback on Specific Performance

Verbal or qualitative feedback can be confusing if it is not specific or based on behavior. Focusing on specific behaviors or events helps the recipient of the feedback to take corrective action. Customers who complain about poor service in general are not providing enough information to help you resolve their complaints. Team members who complain about a teammate's "bad attitude" will likely only contribute to the bad feelings. Focusing on the specific behaviors that contribute to these impressions provides actionable feedback. Use questioning techniques to uncover the real concerns. What do our clerks do that you feel is poor service? What could I do differently to make you believe I am committed to this team?

When giving feedback keep these general guidelines in mind:
- Ask if the person is open to some feedback before beginning.

- Confirm that it is a good time to talk.

- Begin by describing the specific situation you want to talk about and explaining why it is important to you.

- Avoid red-flag words such as incompetent, lazy, and so on.

- Try to begin your statements with I instead of you. Starting a conversation with you can sound accusative even when you don't mean to be.

- Use "tell me" statements instead of direct questions to sound less confrontational. "Tell me what happened" instead of "Why did you do that?"

- Stick to observable facts and don't make assumptions about the other person's motives.

- Paraphrase what the other person says from time to time to show that you are listening and to get confirmation of your understanding.

- In most cases, you should let the other person respond after each of your comments. Listen actively so the other person knows that you are hearing and understanding.

- Maintain the self-esteem of the other person by acknowledging his or her worth and contribution.

- Focus on the future rather than the past.

- Try to let the other person come up with the solution so he or she will be motivated to carry it out.

Ask for Clarification

If you can't interpret the data because they are contradictory or conflicting, the safest strategy is to simply get more information. If, for example, the feedback indicates that half your customers love you and the other half are about to drop you, you should go back and find out the cause of this discrepancy. What specifically makes some customers so happy? What could you be doing differently to please those who are unhappy? Sometimes conflicting feedback is very useful because it uncovers important learning situations. You should use the conflicting data to identify potential improvements. Focus groups (small groups of customers gathered together to give you feedback and react to new ideas) and one-on-one interviews are the most common methods of getting specific, anecdotal feedback.

3. Employees Don't Know How to Act on the Data

Getting data to employees is often not sufficient. Many times employees don't know what to do with all the information they receive. You may understand that you need to lower your blood pressure, for example, but there's nothing to assure you that you know how to do it. Even if your organization has created effective information-sharing systems and closed feedback loops, your workforce may still need help translating that data into productive actions. Until an organization develops the discipline of reviewing and analyzing data on a regular basis at every level, systematic continuous improvement will be difficult to achieve.

Employees don't know how to act on the data

- Structure your data review.
- Develop a regular review/planning process.
- Get outside your box.

Structure Your Data Review

Many employees, especially those new to data analysis, are unsure of how to process feedback. Share this simple four-step process for examining and acting on feedback:

1. Review and assess. Examine the feedback and explore your reactions to it. Is it satisfactory feedback? Does it reveal problems? How closely does it meet your goals? If there are problems, which are of highest priority? This last question helps the work group focus its energies.

2. Determine root causes. Whether the feedback is good or bad, you should understand the causes. If the feedback is good, you will want to know what you need to do more of in order to maintain or improve the results. If the feedback is negative, you will need to know where to perform problem solving for the highest leverage.

3. Action plan. After completing the first two steps, you will need to determine your next steps. If the causes of the data cannot be explained, you will need to design an experiment to learn more about your processes. If the data revealed problems, you will need to design and implement solutions to improve results. If the feedback was good, you will want to identify what you can do to achieve the next level of excellence.

4. Check effectiveness. Check that your actions have had the desired results. Adjust your plan as needed and reenter the process again at Step 1.

For more information on team problem-solving and design of experiments, see *An Introduction to Team-Approach Problem Solving* by Jones and McBride and Montgomery's *Design and Analysis of Experiments*.

Develop a Regular Review/Planning Process

The structured process described above is not meant for use only when there is a problem or aberration in feedback data. Organizations need to be disciplined in their use of feedback and make the examination of data a regularly occurring event. The process described above provides a useful outline for business planning meetings. Basing business planning on feedback data assures the relevancy of planning decisions and discourages decision making based on hunches. Conduct an annual business-planning meeting that uses past performance data to establish new goals. Then follow the format described in the preceding section to structure quarterly meetings (or more frequently if needed) to review progress and design corrective or improvement actions. For a complete description of one method, see Chapter 9 in Hitchcock and Willard's *Why Teams Can Fail and What to Do about It*.

Get Outside Your Box

Many times work groups are hampered by their myopic view of things. They can look at information and not see the possibilities for innovative action. When we are accustomed to doing a job a certain way, it becomes very hard to conceive of truly creative innovations. Consider some of these strategies for generating creative solution options to your team's problems.

- Conduct brainstorming sessions. Adhere strictly to brainstorming rules (go for volume, no evaluation, build on earlier ideas, be "off the wall"). Sometimes it's helpful to set minimums (no discussion until we have at least 30 ideas).

- Begin problem-solving sessions with creativity-inspiring warm-up activities (e.g., give participants a familiar object and ask them to generate 12 new uses for it).

- Go off site. Sometimes it helps to get people away from familiar surroundings. The best results are usually achieved if you can go someplace that is informal and fun.

- Invite outsiders to join you. Some of the most creative ideas are inspired by people who don't know anything about your work.

- Get your customers' perspective. If you can't literally invite them to participate, at least put yourself in their shoes and think about what they would like.

- Start at the end. Begin with the desired outcome and work backwards to explore as many options as possible for achieving that end. Xerox developed its most progressive copier by letting go of the assumption that the original document should not be moved. It focused instead on the outcome of speedy copying and collating.[1]

- Assume the impossible. Ignore all the "yeah, but's" for awhile and design the fantasy solution. Then ask what it would take to create it.

---

1. David Kearns and David Nadler, *Prophets in the Dark,* New York: Harper Business, 1992.

Unless you understand a job thoroughly, it is difficult to design feedback systems and measures that will provide relevant information. For those on the receiving end, getting feedback from uninformed sources can be confusing and sometimes distracting. We roll our eyes when our doctors tell us to reduce the stress in our lives. It's easy for them to say because they know nothing about what we do. As in this example, it is all too tempting to ignore this kind of feedback, but ignoring feedback from any source is generally bad practice. Instead you should help people make the best use of the data that they get. Here are three strategies that address different facets of this problem.

The people who give the feedback don't understand the job

- Train employees to give feedback.
- Establish customer-supplier relationships.
- Be specific in your request for feedback.

Train Employees to Give Feedback

In most organizations employees receive feedback from their manager or supervisor. One of the biggest problems with this approach is that these supervisors are often out of touch with the jobs they're assessing. They may not have performed the job themselves for years, or may never have performed it in the first place. Where this is the case, workers may want to add a peer review process to the appraisal system so that they are assured of getting the kind of feedback they most need to improve their technical job performance.

Peer review may be done informally or it may be designed into the official review system. You may choose to limit feedback to technical performance issues or broaden it to include team or interpersonal performance. However it is handled, be sure to establish guidelines in advance for how it will be done as well as how often it will be done. It is also a good idea to provide training on giving and receiving behavior-focused feedback before you implement this strategy. Here are some general feedback tips:

- Ask if the person is open to some feedback before beginning.

- Confirm that it is a good time to talk.

- Begin by describing the specific situation you want to talk about and explaining why it is important to you.

- Avoid red-flag words such as incompetent or lazy.

- Try to begin your statements with I instead of you. Starting a conversation with you can sound accusative even when you don't mean to be.

- Use "tell me" statements instead of direct questions to sound less confrontational. "Tell me what happened" instead of "Why did you do that?"

- Stick to observable facts and don't make assumptions about the other person's motives.

- Paraphrase what the other person says from time to time to show that you are listening and to get confirmation of your understanding.

- In most cases, you should let the other person respond after each of your comments. Listen actively so the other person knows that you are hearing and understanding.

- Maintain the self-esteem of the other person by acknowledging his or her worth and contribution.

- Focus on the future rather than the past.

- Try to let the other person come up with the solution so he or she will be motivated to carry it out.

Establish Customer-Supplier Relationships

Where one functional group supplies feedback reports to another, differences in professional perspectives and technical jargon can create misunderstandings and confusions. For example, an accounting department that supplies financial reports to a line team is likely to create the kind of report only another accountant can read. If this is the case, employees should establish a customer-supplier relationship with those providing the feedback. The employees should make their needs clear to the people providing the data. Use the following points as an outline for clarifying your data needs:

- Share your key goals/measures (e.g., control costs).

- Frame specific questions that relate to those goals (e.g., What are our direct costs for the quarter? How does that compare to the previous quarter? What were our five biggest line items?).

- Suggest a reporting format (e.g., bar charts comparing this quarter's expenses to last, Pareto diagram of ranked expenses, a narrative summary describing key trends).

Be Specific in Your Request for Feedback

Feedback from customers, internal or external, is critical to any work unit. Often, though, customers have little understanding of the job and frequently make unrealistic requests. Auto manufacturers, for example, have heard conflicting demands from their customers—build a car that is light, fuel efficient, *and* safe.

As discussed in previous sections, learn to ask for specific feedback. The car manufacturers might ask, Which safety feature is more important to you, air bags or antilock brakes? You can begin to educate your customers and manage their expectations in the way that you ask for feedback. Car manufacturers may phrase their question this way: Heavier cars tend to be safer but get lower gas mileage. Would you be willing to trade fuel efficiency for safety?

The "house of quality" process can help you analyze and prioritize customer feedback. For more information on this strategy, see the article called "The House of Quality" by Hauser and Clausing.

Ideally feedback should be used for learning and continuous improvement. Sometimes, though, what we hear is not easy to take and prompts us to get defensive. (I can't lose weight because my metabolism is slow.) When the members of your organization get unpleasant feedback, they too may resort to whining and blaming: It's the sales department's fault. It keeps promising deliveries that we can't make. The source of the problem may be in the way that feedback is used or the way in which it is delivered. Try these strategies to mitigate the blaming tendency.

The feedback contributes to conflict and finger-pointing.

- Use feedback for learning.
- Ensure effective communication skills.
- Focus on solutions.

Use Feedback for Learning

Teams often run into trouble when feedback is used primarily for determining rewards or advancement. Performance evaluations, for example, are often the basis for making decisions regarding merit increases and promotions. This approach to analyzing feedback invariably leads to competition within the unit. People who ostensibly are working together toward a common goal are pitted against each other trying to make their own numbers look best. Shift the focus instead to learning. There is something to be learned from every piece of feedback a team or individual receives. Use positive feedback to celebrate and continue the learning process and critical feedback to initiate problem solving. Each team and each individual on a team should ask of any feedback they receive: What does this imply that I/we could learn to do better? Continuous improvement philosophy is based on the notion that nothing and no one is perfect, that everything can be improved.

Ensure Effective Communication Skills

Frequently the way feedback is delivered pushes more emotional buttons than the content of the message. Data presented in an accusatory way pushes people to feel defensive. Data presented as a team challenge, on the other hand, encourages people to focus on solutions. Part of an effective feedback system includes training in both giving and receiving feedback. Some very basic skills include focusing on performance and choosing words care-fully to avoid red-flag terms or unnecessary exaggeration. An open honest climate contributes to effective feedback. Managers can contribute to this climate by asking for feedback about themselves. Their good faith effort to listen non-defensively and take action on what they learn will model honesty for the rest of the work group.

When giving feedback keep these guidelines in mind:
- Ask if the person is open to some feedback before beginning.

- Confirm that it is a good time to talk.

- Begin by describing the specific situation you want to talk about and explaining why it is important to you.

- Avoid red-flag words such as incompetent or lazy.

- Try to begin your statements with I instead of you. Starting a conversation with you can sound accusative even when you don't mean to be.

- Use "tell me" statements instead of direct questions to sound less confrontational. "Tell me what happened" instead of "Why did you do that?"

- Stick to observable facts and don't make assumptions about the other person's motives.

- Paraphrase what the other person says from time to time to show that you are listening and to get confirmation of your understanding.

- In most cases, you should let the other person respond after each of your comments. Listen actively so the other person knows that you are hearing and understanding.

- Maintain the self-esteem of the other person by acknowledging his or her worth and contribution.

• Focus on the future rather than the past.

• Try to let the other person come up with the solution so he or she will be motivated to carry it out.

Focus on Solutions

 When analyzing or reviewing feedback data (especially negative feedback), keep in mind that important quality tenet: 80 percent of problems are systems problems, not people problems. Steer the conversation away from who, and focus on what and how. Good problem-solving techniques focus on examining facts, understanding discrepancies between what is and what should be, uncovering root causes, and action planning for future success. Getting the work group to adhere to this process should discourage expending energy on blame and finger pointing.

For more information, see *The Quality Toolbox* by Nancy Tague.

11 Rewards

We reinforce and reward the wrong things.

We'd like to think that good health is its own reward. Many of us, however, frequently need extra incentives to stick with our diets and exercise regimes. Lose those extra 10 pounds, and you reward yourself with new clothes. Organizations also need reinforcement systems that reward healthy performance. Rewards can be an effective means to shape behavior and focus energies. If rewards and reinforcements are aligned with the organization's goals, then they make a strong contribution to progress and competitiveness. Where they are misaligned or absent altogether, organizations flounder, or worse, get drawn down an unintended and unproductive path. Consider your own organization's reward or reinforcement practices including compensation, bonuses, nonmonetary rewards, informal reinforcement, recognition, and appraisal systems and see if any of the common problems listed below are evident.

Symptoms

The only time we hear anything is when something's gone wrong. (1, 2)

We reward the wrong behavior. (1, 2)

We reinforce one behavior but end up seeing something else. (1, 2)

Our reward system has no impact on motivation. (3, 4)

People don't seem to value or care about our rewards. (3, 4, 5, 6)

People don't feel valued or rewarded. (3, 5)

Rewards seem unfair. (5)

Causes

1. We don't know what to reward.

2. We don't recognize our inconsistencies.

3. We don't know what people find rewarding.

4. Employees feel no control over outcomes or rewards.

5. Employees perceive our reward system as unfair.

6. We can't change the system.

1. We Don't Know What to Reward

Many times organizations inadvertently reward the wrong things. Focusing all the attention on production, for example, frequently encourages line workers to pass unacceptable product down line in an effort to keep their numbers high. Sometimes organizations simply fail to reward anything consistently because they are unclear about what is important. If this is the case in your organization, consider one of the following strategies.

We don't know what to reward

- Tie rewards to the organization's vision.
- Tie rewards to the organization's key measures.

Tie Reinforcement to the Organization's Vision

The easiest and surest way to focus your reward system is to tie it to your vision statement. Revisit your organization's vision. (If you don't have one see Chapter 1.) What does your vision talk about: providing the fastest turn-around time in the industry; producing the most durable product on the market; or, maintaining long-term relationships with your customers. Whatever its content, it should clearly identify what is of utmost importance to the organization. Rewarding performance that links directly to these issues will encourage value-added behavior more than any rhetoric. For more information, see *Strategic Pay* by Edward Lawler.

Tie Reinforcement to the Organization's Key Measures

In addition to examining your vision, you should also study your organization's key measures. (If you don't have any see Chapter 8.) These measures should be a more specific expression of your vision. If your key measures focus on product durability, then your reinforcement system should reward performance that meets or exceeds goals for product shelf life, return or repair rates, or stress-test results. Federal Express, for example, has identified three key measures for which every employee is accountable: people, service, and profits. The people component is reflected in the feedback each person is given by employees or peers on their performance as a manager or team player. The service component is based on feedback from customers. Profit, of course, is a financial measure for the specific portion of the organization to which an employee is attached. For more information on establishing measures see *Vital Signs* by Steven Hronec.

All too often organizations neglect to align their systems for high performance. A good example are companies that espouse and measure one thing (team work, quality, customer satisfaction) and then reward and reinforce another (individual effort, production rate, sales volumes). In our culture we talk a lot about the importance of good health and even conscientiously track health statistics, but much of our admiration and adoration is saved for people who are under weight or surgically altered. If you think this might be the case in your organization, consider one or more of the following strategies to break this cycle.

We don't recognize our inconsistencies

- Compare your talk with your walk.
- Observe performance or common practices.
- Survey employees.

Compare Your Talk with Your Walk

Take a critical look at what the organization claims to value and compare that to what it actually rewards. Begin by examining your "talk," as expressed in your vision and key measures (see previous section). Then look hard at what you really acknowledge. Do you reward line workers for meeting production quotas, or do they get the accolades for achieving new levels of quality (even when production levels are flat or low)? Do you preach employee involvement but then punish mistakes? Do you say managers should be empowering but still expect them to know everything that goes on?

Study your rewards process as well. What kinds of rewards (perks, bonuses, prizes, promotions, verbal recognition) do you have, and what are the criteria for earning them? Do you claim to value empowering managers and then promote people into management positions based on their seniority instead of their coaching skills?

Frequently our practices for reinforcing are so subtle and ingrained that they are hard to detect. If this is the case, try one of the following two strategies for uncovering inconsistencies.

Observe Performance or Common Practices

Sometimes the best way to discover inconsistencies in your reinforcement system is simply by observing your outcomes. As Arthur Jones said, "Organizations are perfectly designed to get the results they get." If your results are not what you expect or claim to want, the problem is likely an inconsistency in your measurement/reward systems. If line workers are consistently brushing off customer requests or complaints in spite of your speeches about quality service, it is likely that there is something in your reinforcement system that encourages them to do so. Though we are often tempted to blame the performers, in reality (as the late Edwards Deming pointed out) 80 percent of the time the problem is in the system, not the employees. This strategy may best be accomplished by employing someone from outside the organization who can examine your organization objectively. For more information on this issue, see Edgar Schein's book *Organizational Culture and Leadership*.

Survey Employees

If you are unable to ferret out the inconsistencies yourself, simply ask employees what their perceptions are. Consider using the following questions in your survey.
- What do you think management expects of you?
- What do you think you would have to do to get recognized (rewarded, promoted, nominated for award, etc.)?
- What is the secret to succeeding in this organization?

For more information or ideas on this topic see the Bureau of National Affairs publication called *Changing Pay Practices: New Developments in Employee Compensation*. See also *Measuring Customer Satisfaction: Development and Use of Questionnaires* by Bob Hayes.

3. We Don't Know What People Find Rewarding

Wou may have every intention of reinforcing your true values and then miss the mark because you have misinterpreted what your employees value as a reward. Unless the recipients want what you offer, your reward will have little value as an incentive. Before you design an incentive system, consider the following strategies.

We don't know what people find rewarding

- Check your assumptions.
- Survey employees.
- Be prepared to individualize rewards.

Check Your Assumptions

When asked what they think would be the 10 most important motivators for their employees, supervisors will most often put money at the top of the list. When employees are asked the same thing, money usually comes in somewhere around seventh. Many times the fault in reward systems is that they are based on false assumptions about what people find rewarding. This may be due to cultural, gender, or age differences between the people giving the reward and those receiving it. Another strong contributing factor is our blind faith in behavioral theory. If we want to manipulate behavior, we either offer the promise of a reward or the threat of punishment. Some credible research, however, disputes this paradigm and suggests that people are most motivated by the opportunity to satisfy their personal goals. Offering employees a choice of projects is likely to produce much better results that bribing them to take on extra duties. The moral here is to never assume your perceptions of a prize are the same as the person receiving it. For an excellent treatise on rewards and incentives, see Alfie Kohn's *Punished by Rewards*.

Survey Employees

Since you cannot rely on your assumptions about what people value, your safest plan is to ask them. We don't recommend just asking people what they want or what they consider valuable. The question is too broad and leaves too much room for absurdity or sarcasm. Another flaw in this approach is that it doesn't focus sufficiently on your desired outcome—improved performance. Ask instead, What would encourage you to be more productive (or creative or quality focused, etc.)? A way to simplify this survey process is to distribute cards that ask employees to complete one or more of a set of incomplete sentences like the ones that follow:

• At work I feel really proud when . . .

• This would be a great place to work if . . .

• I would do a better job if . . .

Sort the responses into four categories: 1) monetary rewards, 2) nonmonetary tangible rewards, 3) recognition, and 4) other.

Be Prepared to Individualize Rewards

Although the survey approach is sure to get you the most valid and reliable data about what people value as rewards, you are also likely to get a wide range of responses. At first blush this may seem to complicate what was originally a simple system. You can, with a little effort, allow for a good deal of individualization in your reinforcement system. The easiest approach is to use your survey results to identify a concise set of options. You can present these options as a menu and allow employees to select their preferences from the list. If you are willing to be even more flexible, you could simply establish a set of parameters (dollar or authority limit) and allow recipients to suggest rewards of their own design. A good source for ideas is Bob Nelson's *1001 Ways to Reward Employees*.

4. Employees Feel No Control over Outcomes or Rewards

Nothing is more frustrating for employees (or organizations for that matter) than having a reward system over which they have no control. In fact, when employees don't believe that they have the power to "ring the bell," their attitude virtually defeats the purpose of reinforcement. If it will be possible for you to redesign your reward and recognition system, consider implementing some of the following strategies as part of your plan.

Employees feel no control over outcomes or rewards

- Collaboratively design realistic goals.
- Shorten the line of sight.
- Focus on controllable variables.

Collaboratively Design Realistic Goals

Employees may feel impotent if their rewards are tied to unrealistic goals. Enter the CEO who proclaims the organization will shoot for zero defects. Nice thought, but in most industries it is completely unrealistic. If the brass ring is too far out of reach, perhaps no one will even try to grab it. Most employees want to do a good job and will naturally set stretch goals for themselves. Make use of this human trait and involve the members of your organization in establishing realistic yet challenging goals. Depending on the culture of your organization, employees may set low goals at first to ensure they meet them. Accept their initial goals as a show of good faith. Once they reach those goals, celebrate and then ask if they think they can improve their results next time. They will likely rise to the challenge.

Shorten the Line of Sight

Another common flaw in reward systems is that they reward employees for factors too far removed from their span of control. Profit sharing is a good example. In this system high performers may be penalized for the lower performance of groups over which they have no control. Instead, focus rewards on the primary functional unit (PFU). The PFU is the smallest autonomous work unit, like a plant site or agency. Focusing rewards on the performance of the PFU puts the control for achieving them within reach of its members. This sense of control is further strengthened if employees participate in the PFU plan-

ning process and report on how they are contributing to the unit's results. At the same time management should report regularly to all employees on the unit's performance against goals and measures. For more information about PFUs, see Chapter Eight in *Why Teams Can Fail and What to Do about It* by Hitchcock and Willard.

Focus on Controllable Variables

Even if you shorten the line of sight by focusing consequences on the outputs of the PFU, you must still be careful to measure and reward those factors that employees can control. Production levels, for example, are often more a factor of sales than of the efficiency of the production line. Instead of measuring total volume, consider measuring the production line's ability to respond at peak levels. For more information see Robert Doyle's book *Gain Management* or Thomas Wilson's *Innovative Reward Systems for the Changing Workplace.*

5. Employees Perceive Our Reward System as Unfair

In organizations people expect to receive equal treatment for equal performance. When this doesn't happen, you can anticipate a number of negative consequences: performance may drop, reward systems become useless, trust is eroded. Most people will point to an inconsistent reward system as an indicator of hypocrisy. If employees perceive your reward or reinforcement systems as inequitable, try implementing some of these strategies.

Employees perceive our reward system as unfair

- Make standards public.
- Create a balanced reward system.
- Implement a 360° appraisal system.
- Establish fixed compensation ratios.
- Give control over rewards to employees.
- Go back to fundamentals.

Make Standards Public

Sometimes people will perceive a system as unfair because they don't understand how it works. Making public your criteria for receiving rewards will go a long way to dispelling any misunderstandings. Once you go public, be sure that you consistently adhere to your own publicly proclaimed rules.

Create a Balanced Reward System

Reward and recognition systems that are too narrowly focused will often be perceived as unfair. A well-balanced system is one that demonstrates each of the following principles:

- The company gives rewards to a variety of employees from across all levels, functions, and disciplines.

- The company gives a mixture of rewards—from formal incentive programs to informal, spontaneous recognition.

- The company gives recognition and rewards immediately (or very soon) after the event that is being rewarded.

- The company attempts to reward people in a fashion with which they are comfortable and that has meaning to them.

- The company gives rewards, and especially recognition, frequently and generously.

For more information on building a comprehensive recognition system see Joan Klubnik's book *Rewarding and Recognizing Employees*.

Implement a 360° Appraisal System

Employees frequently feel disadvantaged because their rewards are determined solely by their supervisors. Two problems arise in this system. First it puts all the power for determining whether an employee is rewarded or reinforced into the hands of one person. Second, that one person may not be in the best position to evaluate the employee. (See Chapter 10 on feedback.) Implementing a 360° appraisal system can resolve both of these problems. In these systems employees are appraised by their supervisors, their peers, anyone who reports to them, and sometimes their customers. This provides a much more comprehensive picture of performance and prevents the biases of one person from carrying undue weight. Be prepared to first provide training on how to give as well as respond to feedback.

Establish Fixed Compensation Ratios

Disparity is another source of inequity in reward systems. In some organizations top-level managers receive salaries and bonuses that are as much as 50 times higher than the lowest paid employee in the organization. From the bottom it's difficult to understand what a manager or CEO can do that is 50 times more valuable than the person who actually makes the product. In response to this inequality, some organizations have instituted fixed ratios that keep this disparity from becoming to extreme. Some progressive organizations hold the salaries of the highest paid leader to no more than seven times the salary of the lowest paid employee. If this seems too narrow a range, consider the ratio of 9:1 held by many Japanese companies.

For more information see *Strategic Pay* by Edward Lawler.

Give Control over Rewards to Employees

This strategy takes the 360° appraisal system one step further and puts the authority for granting awards into the hands of employees. This idea can be simple or taken to radical extremes. To illustrate the simple side, one organization printed index cards with the company logo and distributed them widely throughout the organization. Employees at all levels used the cards to write thank you notes, "nice work," invitations, and announcements to each other. More daring are the organizations that allot each team a certain amount of money or resources specifically for the purpose of purchasing rewards for teammates or others in the organization. A few organizations have gone so far as to give team members authority to conduct formal performance appraisals, grant time off, and even decide on their own compensation. You will need to think through your own comfort level around this strategy and assure yourself that your company's employees are prepared to take on new responsibilities.

Go Back to Fundamentals

Reinforcement and compensation systems can get very complicated, especially when they must work within union contracts or civil service structures. When everything is getting muddled, take a step back and consider your system in light of two basic compensation principles. The first is that people should be paid the fair market value for their expertise. The second is that all employees should feel that they are sharing in the wealth. Salary studies (perhaps conducted by the employees themselves, as is done in parts of Semco in Brazil) will help you check your practices against the first principle. In the case of the second, examine how profits are used and study such options as gain sharing, profit sharing, or even employee ownership.

For more information see *Strategic Pay* by Edward Lawler.

6. We Can't Change the System

You may fully recognize all the drawbacks to your reward system but have no authority to change it. Union contracts, civil service classifications, or parent company policies may determine the practices that you must use. If this is the case, you should look for ways to leverage informal opportunities to reinforce the performance you are after. Presented here are some short term, relatively quick-fix solutions and ideas. For more satisfactory, long-term solutions, study some of the strategies described in Part V.

We can't change the system.

- Increase verbal/informal rewards.
- Allow for more job control.

Increase Verbal/Informal Rewards

Even where you cannot impact official compensation or reward systems, few organizational policies prevent you from implementing informal recognition practices such as employee-of-the-month awards, write-ups in the organization's newsletter, or a small party held in someone's honor. Seldom do employees think they get enough acknowledgment from their supervisors or their peers for the work that they do. Catching people doing something right is the easiest and often the most effective form of reinforcement. Try some of these easy ideas:

- Make blank cards (or cards printed with company logo or an opening line) available to everyone to jot down a quick compliment or good-job note to someone else (peer, staff, or boss).

- Make a point of recognizing someone at each regular meeting.

- Pass a trophy around your unit from person to person in recognition of some specific behavior or performance. You might even make the person who currently has the trophy responsible for choosing the next recipient.

For more ideas refer to *1001 Ways to Reward Employees* by Bob Nelson.

Allow for More Job Control

Sometimes the best reward is more control over the job or simply the opportunity to see something through to completion. We all feel intrinsic satisfaction when we can determine what kinds of assignments we will take on as well as how to fulfill them. However, we inadvertently punish people by arbitrarily reassigning them to new tasks before they have had a chance to experience the satisfaction of completing a whole project or product. Whenever possible, allow people to choose or design their own assignments. If they are able to achieve efficiencies in their own workloads, you can reward them by allowing them to take on a special project of their own choosing. Leveraging people's interests and enthusiasm in this way generally results in a win–win situation. If you try this strategy keep the following job satisfaction elements in mind:[1]

- Variety—A variety of tasks to perform.

- Importance—Tasks must seem important.

- Wholeness—Employees should complete a whole piece of work.

- Autonomy—Employees should have control over planning, scheduling, and evaluating the task.

- Feedback—Employees should receive performance feedback from the task itself.

---

1. Richard Hackman and Greg Oldham, *Work Redesign*, New York: Addison Wesley, 1980.

PART IV PEOPLE

As knowledge work replaces physical work as the primary source of competitive advantage, people become increasingly important. For decades many executives have mouthed the mantra, Our people are our greatest asset, but few have demonstrated a commitment to it. In the future those who do not internalize this belief are doomed. Your competitors can buy the same technology, reverse engineer your products, and undercut your prices. In this knowledge-based economy, your only sustainable competitive advantage is leveraging the knowledge and passion of your employees.

Most people want to do a good job and want to contribute to the success of the organization, but four common illnesses get in their way.

Personality and core abilities	We don't seem to have the right people to get the job done.	Chapter 12
Motivation	What employees want and the organization needs are incompatible.	Chapter 13
Knowledge and skills	People don't know how to do it right.	Chapter 14
Shared learning	We are missing opportunities because we don't share what we know.	Chapter 15

12 Personality and Core Abilities

We don't seem to have the right people to get the job done.

Employees bring with them many things that an organization cannot easily change. Their basic personality and their values are nearly impossible to affect. Similarly, employees lacking basic skills such as reading, math, and the ability to learn will be at a significant and persistent disadvantage until or unless they correct their deficiencies.

In addition to skills, people also bring their interests to the work place. They like to do certain things and not others, and they are driven to find an outlet for their interests. For example, a power company lineman scored high in both the realistic area (liking to work with things) and the artistic area (liking creative work) on an interest assessment. Certainly, his position fulfilled the realistic category. When asked how he satisfied his artistic longing, the bulky man held out his beefy, weathered hands and said, "Oh, I play the piano when I go home."

People are driven to express their interests. When jobs match employees' interests, they are far more likely to be motivated and satisfied with their work. If a person's interests are not satisfied at work, she or he will seek opportunities outside of work. In some cases, people come to work only so they can pay for what they really want to do outside of work. This situation is a terrible waste of human potential.

With this information in mind, organizations should screen applicants for critical abilities and create a good fit between the employees and their working environment.

Review the symptoms listed on the next page and identify the most likely cause of your difficulties.

Symptoms	Causes
Symptoms	**Causes**
Employees are bored. (1)	1. Inappropriate match of employee to the job.
Employees are not performing well. (1, 2, 3)	2. Missing basic work skills.
Employees don't seem to care about work. (1, Part III)	3. Missing appropriate work ethic.
Employees engage in unhealthy conflict. (4)	4. Personality clashes between people.
Employees engage in group think (everyone appears to agree but not all points of view are being considered). (5)	5. Not enough diversity on the team.
	(See also Part III)
Your decisions do not take into account the cultural diversity of your customers. (5)	

Now turn to the cause that seems most likely to be the source of your problem.

1. Inappropriate Match of Employee to the Job

To maximize employee performance and satisfaction, an employee should be carefully matched to the position. Almost any task will be disliked by some people and enjoyed by others. Many performance problems can be solved by changing jobs.

For decades, our organizations have convinced employees that getting ahead means moving up the corporate ladder. This belief sometimes leads to the Peter Principle: people being promoted beyond their level of competence or interest. A scientist is promoted to manager of research and development only to discover she doesn't like managing. The best sales representative is promoted to sales manager only to discover that he's better at selling than he is at managing.

This situation is a terrible waste of human resources and is often damaging to self-esteem. The solution is to return the employees to positions where their gifts and interests are assets, not liabilities. Find a good match between the organization's needs and the individual's gifts and interests.

> **Inappropriate match of employee to the job**

- Improve your selection/hiring process.
- Offer career development training and assessments.
- Separate tasks by interest area.

Improve Your Selection/Hiring Process

Prevention is the best medicine. Ideally, you should screen out people who are not a good fit with the organization before they join. Many organizations are including work-related tasks as part of the hiring process. When Boeing opened a high-involvement plant in Spokane, Washington, its selection procedure involved four weeks of training *before* a candidate could be hired and at least one-quarter of that time involved developing the applicant's team skills.[1] If you think the cost of such a selection process is high, consider the costs of making the wrong decision!

Some organizations are finding that computers are helping to get honest responses from applicants. For example, Neiman Marcus uses computers to screen applicants before interviews and has been amazed at the honesty of some of the responses.[2] For more information, see "Cyberinterviews Combat Turnover" by David Stamps.

Offer Career Development Training and Assessments

Few employees have conducted a thorough analysis of their interests and skills, and even fewer know how to match these to jobs. In today's turbulent climate with entire careers becoming extinct while new ones are created, all employees need to know how to match their interests to the available work.

---

1. Brown, Hitchcock, and Willard, *Why TQM Fails and What to Do about It.*
2. David Stamps, "Cyberinterviews Combat Turnover," *Training,* April 1995, pp. 43–47.

Amoco's excellent career development process has been used as a benchmark for other organizations. It includes required training for supervisors to help employees assess their skills, voluntary training for all employees, a worldwide job-posting system, a network of career advisors, and a worldwide directory of Amoco employees and their skills.[3] See "Flat and Happy" by Marc Hequet for more information.

Career development usually entails assessing an individual's strengths and interests. The most commonly used assessments include the self-directed search, the strong interest inventory, the career assessment inventory, and the career maturity inventory. Make these tests available to all employees and provide managers with basic training in the concepts so they can help direct employees. (See *Wishcraft* by Barbara Sher, *What Color Is Your Parachute* by Richard Bolles, and *Making Vocational Choices* by John Holland.)

Separate Tasks by Interest Area

Sometimes jobs require employees to have opposing, mutually exclusive interests. Some jobs, such as writing books, require people to work by themselves for extended periods and then become outgoing personalities for talk shows and the lecture circuit. Others, such as nuclear power-plant operators, are fraught with drudgery and boredom, punctuated with moments of terror. It is difficult to find one individual who will excel at both extremes. You severely limit the potential pool of applicants if your job design includes opposing interest areas.

---

3. Marc Hequet, "Flat and Happy," *Training,* April 1995, p. 31.

One solution is to analyze the jobs in terms of the interests or personalities necessary to perform the tasks. Then separate the tasks into more logical groupings and redefine the positions based on this analysis.

Use these categories to analyze the job and employee. Most people and jobs represent a mixture of characteristics.

- Realistic—Practical and action oriented; prefers working with things, not people or concepts.

- Investigative—Inquisitive and analytical; prefers research and analysis; conceptual; tolerant of long time frames.

- Artistic—Creative, intuitive; believes rules are made to be broken.

- Social—People oriented, cooperative, idealistic; wants to help others.

- Enterprising—Entrepreneurial; risk tolerant; willing to lead; persuasive.

- Conventional—Ordered, organized, does things by the book; likes to work with data and numbers.

For more information on these categories, see *Making Vocational Choices: A Theory of Vocational Personalities and Work Environments* by John Holland.

2. Missing Basic Work Skills

Organizations have increasingly complained that their new hires lack basic skills. This is not necessarily a condemnation of our school system. Many organizations are hiring more immigrants who did not attend our schools and for whom English is a second language. Also, work is becoming more complex. Now people need to know how to use computers and understand statistics for many positions. This problem will only get worse in the future, so it is important to have strategies to deal with it.

Many people will go to great lengths to disguise the fact that they are missing basic skills. Job applicants may ask to take the application home (so someone can help them complete it). Employees may resist working in teams because they may be called upon to write on a flip chart or speak in front of a group. One company was sued in part because workers could not read the warning signs on hazardous chemicals; the notices were in English, not the workers' preferred language. The costs associated with the lack of basic skills are enormous.

Missing basic work skills

- Create a partnership with local schools and colleges.
- Screen applicants for basic skills.
- Offer basic-skills training.

Create a Partnership with Local Schools and Colleges

Many organizations are creating partnerships with their local schools and colleges. The organizations can influence the curriculum and perhaps even provide real-world problems for students to solve. Many states are also trying to bridge the abrupt transition from school to work through internships, mentoring, and apprenticeship programs. The following practices are already in use:

• Speak at a school.

• Offer informational interviews.

• Teach a class at school.

• Host student and teacher visits to the workplace.

• Permit students to "shadow" employees.

• Supervise apprentices.

• Mentor students.

• Help design school programs.

• Contract to provide work experience for students and teachers.

Screen Applicants for Basic Skills

Another option is to screen applicants for basic skills. According to a study conducted by the Department of Labor and the American Society for Training and Development, the skills most employers seek fall into seven skill groups:

• Learning to learn.

• Reading, writing, and computation.

• Listening and oral communication.

• Creative thinking, problem solving.

• Self-esteem, goals setting, motivation, personal and career development.

• Interpersonal, negotiation, teamwork.

• Organizational effectiveness.[4]

For many industries, however, screening applicants is not a viable option. As of this writing, unemployment is near historic lows in the United States, partially owing to the economy and partially owing to demographic trends. You may have no choice but to provide basic skills training to your employees.

4. A. Carnevale, L. Gainer, and A. Metlzer. *Workplace Basics: The Skills Employers Want* (Washington DC: ASTD and the Dept. of Labor, 1988).

Offer Basic-Skills Training

 You have several options for providing basic-skills training. You can offer educational assistance and expect employees to pursue this training on their own time. You can also provide workshops on site (taught by consultants, community colleges, or your own instructors) either on or off work time.

Whichever option you choose, be sure to do an adequate assessment of the training needs before paying for any training. A scattershot training approach is rarely effective and is enormously expensive. Second, embed real-world organizational tasks into the curriculum. Have trainees read actual company manuals, write real business letters/reports, or compute statistics on real production data. Third, but most important, be respectful of those who seek basic-skills training. Many people are embarrassed that they lack these skills, so do whatever you can to make acquiring them safe and comfortable. For more information, see *Educating America* by Jack Bowsher.

3. Missing Appropriate Work Ethic

Throughout history, older generations have bemoaned the work ethic (and the music) of the younger generations. Over the decades, what each generation as a whole expects out of work has changed—usually in response to large socioeconomic issues. It is a mistake, however, to assume that kids these days aren't motivated or that they have a bad work ethic. Everyone is motivated by something. And a "bad" work ethic is often an appropriate psychological response to an inhumane workplace.

Consider the experience at NUMMI, a joint venture between General Motors and Toyota. The plant had been shut down for quality and labor problems. When it reopened and showed dramatic improvements, people came from around the country to tour the plant. One touring manager was overheard to say, "Yeah, but your people are different." A NUMMI employee overhearing the comment just shook his head. 85 percent of the workforce were the original employees! The point is that the work environment has a powerful influence on people's behavior. Most people want to do a good job–if they are well-suited to their job and the environment will let them.[5]

Missing appropriate work ethic

- Provide for elements of job satisfaction.
- Align rewards and reinforcements.
- Screen applicants for values and ethics.

---

5. T. Mahoney and J. Deckop, "Y'Gotta Believe: Lessons from American vs Japanese Run US Factories," *Organizational Dynamics*, 21 (Spring 1993), p. 27.

Provide for Elements of Job Satisfaction

If one person in a particular position seems dissatisfied, demotivated, disgruntled, check for a bad job fit or personal problems at home. If you think that the job fit is bad, see the section on inappropriate match of employee to the job earlier in this chapter. If the problem stems from personal issues, refer the individual to counseling.

However, if many people in a position feel unhappy, the job may be poorly designed. Job design is a major factor in employee satisfaction and performance. For employees to enjoy their work, their job must include these five factors:[6]

- Variety—A variety of tasks to perform.

- Importance—Tasks must seem important.

- Wholeness—Employees should complete a whole piece of work.

- Autonomy—Employees should have control over planning, scheduling, and evaluating the task.

- Feedback—Employees should receive performance feedback from the task itself.

In particular, make sure that employees have a voice in matters that affect them. Employees who are not treated well by their employers often find ways to retaliate. Involve your employees in goal setting and planning. Act on their suggestions and make sure they always understand why decisions are made.

---

6. Oldham and Hackman

Align Rewards and Reinforcements

Employees often act counter to the needs of the organization when they are rewarded or reinforced for the wrong things. In one organization, a team was grinding up A-grade lumber to make chips because that's what they were measured on. An organization's systems can create performance problems, and employees often feel torn and resentful about being "forced" to do the wrong thing. See Chapter Eleven if you suspect this is a problem for your company.

Screen Applicants for Values and Ethics

While everyone is motivated, not everyone is motivated to do what's best for the organization. Many organizations are screening applicants for values and ethics by using various assessments which purport to identify an individual's level of honesty, ethical behavior, and the like.

If you choose this option, make sure that the assessments you use have been thoroughly tested and are valid and reliable. Also, seek legal advice on the use of these assessments—how to use them, what to do with the data, how to ensure they do not violate equal opportunity laws, how to limit your exposure to law suits, and so on.

4. Personality Clashes Between People

Today's workplace demands far more interdependence and teamwork. Consequently, personality clashes are even more common. As the stakes are raised and one person's work depends on another's output, opportunities for friction multiply. This situation is exacerbated further by our increasingly diverse workplace.

Personality clashes between people

- Train people in team-building fundamentals.
- Offer diversity training.
- Conduct personality-style assessments.
- Change the membership of the team.

Train People in Team-Building Fundamentals

Some conflict between individuals is normal and healthy. Teams should actively solicit and discuss differing views. How this conflict is handled is paramount, so provide training for everyone on conflict-resolution fundamentals.

Some conflicts arise out of unspoken assumptions or inappropriate behaviors. Creating a set of team agreements or ground rules builds consensus for acceptable behavior. See *The Team Handbook* by Peter Scholtes for tools and techniques.

Also, teams need to understand that conflict is more likely during certain phases of their development. The most common model of team development is form-storm-norm-perform. Usually within a few months of forming a team, people begin to grate on each other. Teams cannot avoid this storm stage, but knowing that it is normal can help them prepare for and weather it. For more information on this model, see "Developmental Sequence in Small Groups" by B. W. Tuckman.

Offer Diversity Training

An organization cannot reach high performance if some of the employees feel disenfranchised and unvalued. As our organizations become more diverse, training on valuing these differences becomes increasingly important. To get the most from their members, teams must know how various cultures deal with conflict, time, and power. Employers must comply with federal laws and learn how to accommodate employees with disabilities. Simply recognizing the assets that each person brings as a result of his or her interests, personality, gender, race, and background helps organizations make the most of their human resources.

The Center for Creative Leadership has developed a seven-dimension model of cultural diversity (only one type of diversity). Discussing the following attributes may be revealing:
- Sources of identity (individual versus collective).
- Methods of achievement (assertive versus supportive).
- Response to authority (equal versus unequal).
- Orientation to opportunity (dynamic versus stable).
- Means of knowledge acquisition (active versus reflective).
- Perspectives on time (scarce versus plentiful).
- Outlook on life (doing versus being).[7]

The following tips are useful for valuing diversity:
- Design training that takes into account the different learning styles of a diverse group.
- Provide diversity training for your workforce.
- Acknowledge and leverage individual differences.
- Create opportunities for different groups of people to work together (cross-functional teams, project teams, problem-solving task forces).
- Assess and examine the impact of bias in your workplace.

---

7. M. Wilson, "The Intercultural Values Questionnaire," *Issues and Observations* 15, no. 1, p. 10.

• Model diversity-valuing skills by openly acknowledging your own misconceptions, seeking information about diversity, and fostering relationships with people who are different from you.[8]

For a good resource of activities and tips, see *The Managing Diversity Survival Guide* by Gardenswartz and Rowe. Also see *Managing Workforce 2000* by Jamieson and O'Mara.

Conduct Personality-Style Assessments

Often employees clash because they have different personality or communication styles. Understanding our differences, with their respective strengths and weaknesses, helps employees to accommodate the needs of others.

You can use numerous assessments. Most are built from a model attributed to Carl Jung that maps personalities on two dimensions: task versus relationship and assertive/risk tolerant/fast paced versus less assertive and less risk-tolerant. This model yields four predominant styles: driver, analyzer, promoter, and supporter. This simple model helps team members to understand their differences, modify their approaches to accommodate different styles, and compensate for an imbalance of styles on the team.

Other, more complex surveys are available. Myers-Briggs, for example, measures on four attributes, yielding 16 personality

categories. See *Gifts Differing* by Isabel and Peter Myers. While these are often excellent, well-validated assessments, we recommend that you begin with ones based on only a few style categories. Unless you have significant time to explore the more complex surveys, the plethora of categories is more likely to overwhelm employees.

Pick a survey that has been validated and provides a simple, useful model for managing everyday interactions. Have all members take the survey before being exposed to the model upon which it is based. After discussing the results, facilitate a discussion on how these personality styles are helping and hindering the team's performance.

Change the Membership of the Team

Some individuals, usually because of negative past interactions, may never work well together. Often the simplest way to resolve personality clashes is to place the warring parties on different teams. However, ask yourself this question before transferring an individual: Will this change simply transfer a problem to a different team? If the individual is likely to work well in a different setting, make the move. However, if the individual needs to resolve other issues, transferring him or her will only postpone learning (making it a potential bandaid). In these cases, the best course is usually to provide counseling to the individual and his or her coworkers to resolve the root cause.

---

8. Adapted from D. Jamieson and J. O'Mara, *Managing Workforce 2000.* (San Francisco: Jossey Bass Publishers, 1991).

5. Not Enough Diversity on the Team

Work groups must walk a fine line between integration and differentiation, between hiring clones and becoming so diverse that alignment is impossible. The need for diversity does not stem so much from affirmative action and EEOC goals. It is a reflection of the global, diverse marketplace. A white American male, no matter how understanding and enlightened, cannot fully understand what it's like to be an African-American female in business, much less the nuances of Japanese culture. Ignorance about cultural differences has caused embarrassing mistakes, such as General Motors trying to sell its Nova in South America (no va means "doesn't go" in Spanish). Perhaps your customers require someone who speaks Korean, Russian, or Portuguese. Diversity is not a nicety; it is a necessity!

A team requires more than cultural and racial diversity. If everyone on the team has similar knowledge, personalities, or interests, the team may not have the necessary resources to perform its task well. If no one on the team is analytical, the team may miss important data. If everyone on the team is analytical, the team may get stuck in analysis paralysis. You need a mix. See "Different from What: Diversity as a Performance Issue" by Jack Gordon.

Not enough diversity on the team

- Use personality style and other critical diversity attributes as selection criteria.

- Create cross-functional teams.

- Rotate team members.

Use Personality Style and Other Critical Diversity Attributes as Selection Criteria

One obvious solution is to identify the critical diversity elements and include them in your selection criteria when an opening appears on the team. Be careful not to run afoul of EEOC law, however. Ask your human resources director or corporate attorney for guidance.

For more information, see *Managing Workforce 2000* by Jamieson and O'Mara.

Create Cross-Functional Teams

An organization may require maximum diversity only on certain tasks—product design, for example. When Boeing designed its 777, it involved people from across the organization as well as its customers. This involvement led them to change many things about the plane, making it easier to service and maintain. People from manufacturing, engineering, and maintenance cooperated to create an optimal design. See "Betting on the 21st Century Jet" by Jeremy Main.

In these situations, a cross-functional, temporary team can design the product/service or solve a specific problem. These teams help to build understanding across parts of the organization.

Rotate Team Members

Another option for increasing the diversity on the team is to rotate new members into the team on a regular basis, usually at specific milestones or at the completion of a project. With a continuous stream of new blood, the team is more likely to get diverse viewpoints over time without having to screen team members for specific attributes. As work becomes more oriented around projects instead of traditional jobs, this option becomes increasingly attractive. See *Liberation Management* by Tom Peters to learn more about the evolution to project work. Also see *Job Shift: How to Prosper in a Workplace without Jobs* or "The End of the Job" both by William Bridges.

13 Motivation

What employees want and what the organization needs are incompatible.

High performance only happens when employees' needs are aligned with those of the organization. An employee's personal motivation—what the individual wants out of work—is not easily affected by the organization. To complicate matters, an employee's motivation tends to change over time. An unmarried 21-year-old will have different needs and expectations than a middle-aged parent with three children clamoring for college. Thus, screening for motivation in the selection process is only a short-term solution.

Organizations must also find ways to engage employees in goal setting and to be flexible in job assignments.

It's important to recognize that you cannot make someone be motivated. Motivation comes from within. All that managers can do is to create an environment where employees' motivations can blossom to the benefit of the organization. (See "One More Time: How Do You Motivate Employees?" by Frederick Herzberg.)

Review the symptoms on the next page and determine the most likely cause of your people problem. Then turn to the cause to identify the appropriate treatment.

Symptoms

Employees seem oblivious to the competitive challenges that face the organization and seem ignorant of the organization's strategy to deal with them. (1)

Employees seem not to care about the direction and needs of the organization. (1, 3, 4, 5)

Rewards and recognition don't seem to be generating the desired behaviors. (2, Chapter 11)

Employees complain about being stuck. (4)

Employees seem unnecessarily stressed. (5)

Employees situation at home has recently changed drastically. (5)

Causes

1. Employees have no input into the direction of the organization.

2. Management doesn't know what employees want.

3. Employees can't see what's in it for them.

4. Career advancement opportunities are limited.

5. Employee's personal needs are not a good fit with the organization or job.

(See also Chapter 11.)

If employees have no influence on the direction of the organization, it is easy for them to become disgruntled. Involving them in establishing the mission and goals provides a forum for them to discover the overlap between the organization's needs and their own. The following three suggestions, then, revolve around discovering and acting on the collective will of employees.

Employees have no input into the direction of the organization

- Establish a shared vision and mission for the organization.
- Involve employees in goal setting and strategy setting.
- Redirect organizational priorities based on the collective will of the employees.

Establish a Shared Vision and Mission for the Organization

In traditional organizations, setting vision and mission was the job of the executives. However, being handed a mission statement just doesn't generate the same ownership or commitment that comes with participating in its creation. It is the process that creates the understanding and energy, not the words on paper. See *Leadership and the New Science* by Margaret Wheatley. See also "Building a Shared Vision" in *The Fifth Discipline* by Peter Senge.

Marvin Weisbord's future-search-conference process can involve many people in creating a preferred future while identifying common ground. These are typically two-day meetings with up to 60 people. The members explore their past, analyze the present, and develop a shared vision for the future. To make this format work, the executives must be comfortable with the openness of this approach. See *Future Search* and *Discovering Common Ground* both by Marvin Weisbord.

For a somewhat more directive option, you might explore Robert Jacobs's real-time strategic-change approach that involves the executives presenting a draft strategy while including many of the elements of a future search. This approach can involve more participants than the search conference and usually takes three days. For more information, see *Real-Time Strategic Change* by Robert Jacobs.

Involve Employees in Goal Setting and Strategy Setting

Management by objectives has been popular for many years. However, this goal-setting method relies on top management to set the direction and leaves it to those lower in the organization to figure out how to meet the goals. This process is too cumbersome, slow, and disempowering to meet the needs of today's organizations.

Employees can be involved in many ways. One option is to modify the planning process so that employees and teams roll their business plans up through the organization. See "The Engine of Empowerment" by Darcy Hitchcock or the chapter on goals and measures in *Why Teams Can Fail* by Hitchcock and Willard. Also see *Liberation Management* by Tom Peters.

Another option is to ask the entire organization (or large segments of it) to define the strategy. See *Real-Time Strategic Change* by Robert Jacobs for such a process. Sometimes, just letting employees decide is the best strategy. For example, Ralph Stayer, owner of Johnsonville Foods, discovered significant advantages to involving employees in some major strategic decisions. He asked his employees whether they should take over production of a competing plant—which led to a 50 percent increase in production! See "How I Learned to Let My Employees Lead" by Ralph Stayer, and *Flight of the Buffalo* by James Belasco and Ralph Stayer.

Redirect Organizational Priorities Based on the Collective Will of the Employees

Some organizations discover through interviews and climate surveys that employees are dissatisfied with the direction of the organization. One organization changed its manufacturing process when it discovered that employees were troubled by the environmental effects. Others have gotten into or out of certain markets or products for the same reasons. Eliminating animal testing, toxic waste, and excess packaging are more than good PR. It helps your employees commit to the organization. Ask your employees what makes them proud about the organization and what doesn't. Then act on what they tell you.

Many organizations put together elaborate reward systems to motivate employees only to discover that employees don't value the rewards. Research has shown that managers often misjudge what employees want and need to be more productive. They often assume that extrinsic motivators like money and promotions are the biggest motivator. However, often intrinsic motivators such as pride, achievement, an opportunity to contribute, and control over the work are more powerful. These intrinsic motivators must be managed differently and often cost the organization nothing.

Management doesn't know what employees want

- Survey employees.
- Give employees control/flexibility over rewards.
- Continually evaluate and improve your recognition programs.

Survey Employees

The best solution is often so simple: Ask employees what they need. Ask them what would help them or encourage them to be more productive. One approach we designed is to give managers a set of cards to distribute to a random sampling of employees. The cards ask the employees to complete one of the following sentences:

• At work, I feel proud when...

• At work, I really get excited when...

• At work, I really wish...

• When I do a really great job, I'd like...

• This could be a much better place to work if only...

The employees write their answers on the back of the cards. Sort the cards into four piles that indicate a desire for (1) monetary rewards, (2) nonmonetary tangible rewards, (3) recognition, and (4) other. Then analyze the cards in each pile. We have done this many times and have consistently discovered that there are usually only a couple cards on the monetary or nonmonetary piles. The bulk of the cards on the remaining two piles fall into three categories: atta-boys (more feedback and verbal recognition), teamwork (why can't we just get along) and control over the work (let me finish the job, decide how to do it, etc.).

Give Employees Control/Flexibility over Rewards

People are motivated by different things and no one system will meet everyone's needs. One solution is to give employees some control over the rewards they get. Here are some of the examples we've seen:

• At a county agency, team members can give one another "Hang 10" awards that are certificates of appreciation. These are posted in the main lobby.

• At a manufacturing company, teams and team members can give recognition awards (such as cups, jackets, pizza parties, etc.) to any other team. An oversight committee helps the team select an appropriate gift/award. The only control is that the individual or team must stand up in an all-employee meeting and explain why they are giving the award. Peer pressure prevents abuse.

• At a defense contractor, team members can be nominated for a customer service all-star award. An internal or external customer nominates an individual for superior customer service. Then the employee's team leader is consulted to determine the most effective way to deliver the recognition award—privately or in public. The customer(s) and the employee's leader arrange a time to surprise the employee and deliver the recognition, which includes a certificate for a dinner for two worth $60.

See *1001 Ways to Reward Employees* by Bob Nelson.

Continually Evaluate and Improve Your Recognition Programs

 Recognition programs typically need to be updated to maintain their effect. Evaluate and improve your programs at least annually. In our opinion, AT&T Universal Card Services (winner of the Malcolm Baldrige Award) and Rubbermaid (listed in *Fortune* magazine's most admired corporation in 1995) have examples of particularly effective programs. Focus on providing a wide variety of rewards, with a balance of team and individual rewards, and change them constantly. See *Bringing out the Best in People* by Aubrey Daniels. See also Chapter 11 for more information on reinforcement.

3. Employees Can't See What's in It for Them

At a large chemical manufacturer, the employees understood why the organization wanted to implement high-performance teams. It'll improve profits and give the CEO a huge bonus, was their explanation. What they couldn't fathom is why they would want to make this change; it looked like a lot of work and involved a lot of personal risk. Everyone is tuned to the same radio station: WIIFM. What's in it for me?

Often, employees can see the benefit a particular change will bring for the organization. However, if they see nothing in it for themselves, they are unlikely to be motivated to support the change. Even impending layoffs can sometimes represent positive changes for employees. Organizations must help employees understand the benefits for them.

Employees can't see what's in it for them

- Conduct shared visioning sessions.
- Survey employees for suggestions.
- Manage personal transitions.
- Make employees owners/ shareholders.

Conduct Shared Visioning Sessions

Employees who participate in developing the vision and plans have an opportunity to build in something for themselves. Marvin Weisbord's future-search-conference process can involve many people in creating a preferred future while identifying common ground. These are typically two-day meetings with up to 60 people. Together, the members explore their past, analyze the present, and develop a shared vision for the future. To make this format work, the executives must be comfortable with the openness of this approach. See *Future Search* and *Discovering Common Ground* both by Marvin Weisbord.

For a somewhat more directive option, you might explore Robert Jacobs's real-time strategic-change approach that involves the executives presenting a draft strategy while including many of the elements of a future search. This approach can involve more participants than the search conference and usually takes three days. For more information, see *Real-Time Strategic Change* by Robert Jacobs.

Survey Employees for Suggestions

If employees cannot be included in the planning of a change, they can at least be polled for ideas of what they would like to see changed. In a team setting, you can use a flip chart or board to create a "gripe list." On a larger scale, one executive of an international training company sends out his questions and suggestions to all employees via e-mail. He says when the replies drop off precipitously, he's close to a good solution.

After polling people for their ideas, the organization can often link the employee's suggestions directly to the planned changes. Before implementing this option, however, it is important to educate employees on the current and future prospects for the organization. *Reengineering Work* by Hammer and Champy has a nice section on writing a case for change that performs this function.

Manage Personal Transitions

Just as the organization must build a case for change, employees can do the same. By analyzing their current situation and future prospects, employees often discover that the change the organization is planning will help them as well. For example, many managers and executives are actively pursuing learning and experience in high-performance principles even though these principles may result in them losing their jobs. Their reason? They will be far more likely to find future work with these skills.

Personal transitions begin with endings—focusing on the losses, not the new opportunities. Organizations must help people through this grieving process to prepare them for the future. Some organizations stage elaborate rituals such as wakes, funerals, and the like. While corny, these rites provide a forum for acknowledging the past and preparing for the future.

William Bridges suggests the following format for group retreats to prepare for a significant change:

- Have public recognition of endings (let participants tell stories, and have food and drink). Then let people go to bed.

- Next morning, allow for the neutral-zone retreat. Have periods of quiet, perhaps fasting, creative exploration, visualization. Then do something totally different.

- Finally, do life and career planning.

See *Managing Transitions: Making the Most from Change* or *Surviving Corporate Transition* by William Bridges.

Make Employees Owners/Shareholders

Employees may resent an environment in which all their efforts go toward making owners and shareholders wealthy. One solution is to make employees owners, as with an employee stock option plan. Avis, United Airlines, and others have found employee ownership an effective means to reenergize their organizations and make them more competitive. One caution: For this plan to work, employees must have more than stock. They must be given significant influence over the direction of the organization. For more information, see *The Great Game of Business* by Jack Stack and the chapter on organizational democracy in *Why Teams Can Fail* by Hitchcock and Willard.

4. Career Advancement Opportunities Are Limited

Opportunities for advancement have always been limited; the pyramid gets narrower toward the top. In recent years delayering has led to extremely flat organizations with even fewer management positions.

The first step to resolving this dilemma is to recognize that we have, to a large extent, created an artificial demand for advancement. Most people do not so much want to move up as to move on. The first violinist probably does not want to become conductor or the director of the concert hall. The engineer may not want to become manager of engineering. Usually, the pursuit of more control and income moves people up the ladder, often to positions that are no longer a good fit with their gifts.

Instead, we must provide opportunities for people to grow: to develop new skills, and to attack new challenges. We must design jobs so that employees do not have to move into management to earn more money or to have more control over their work environment. This section includes several suggestions:

Career advancement opportunities are limited

- Enlarge/enrich the job.
- Encourage lateral transfers.
- Develop career ladders or career webs.
- Design new roles.

Enlarge/Enrich the Job

Enlarging a job increases the variety of tasks. If you enrich the job as well and give employees more control over their work, you can also satisfy another personal need. Look horizontally and vertically. Horizontally, you could add tasks before and after a particular step in a process. For example, an employee could learn how to operate more pieces of equipment that manufacture your product. Vertically, the employee could take on more of the "management" tasks such as planning the work (which affects autonomy as well). Vertical integration usually leads to self-directed teams where employees take on many of the responsibilities of a traditional supervisor. See *Productive Workplaces* by Marvin Weisbord for more information.

Encourage Lateral Transfers

Sometimes people simply need a new experience, a change of venue. Lateral transfers help to build understanding and knowledge across organizational boundaries. One potential drawback of lateral transfers is that performance may dip while the employee learns the new job. However, the payback in employee motivation and understanding of the big picture usually offsets these costs. Note: If moving expenses are involved, make sure that the lateral transfer will benefit the organization significantly.

Develop Career Ladders or Career Webs

Career ladders are helpful where employees do not value moving sideways in an organization. In fields where competency is achieved through years of education and experience, these ladders can help recognize an employee's progress. They allow people to progress in their technical fields instead of having to move into management to earn a higher salary. This approach helps to keep people in positions suited to their personalities instead of promoting people into management. Identify levels of knowledge and contribution in a technical field. Then identify appropriate training and experiences that would lead someone from one level to another. Pay usually increases as an employee moves up the career ladder. In some cases technical employees end up earning more than their managers.

Design New Roles

With a little creativity and flexibility, an organization can often let an employee design a new role. Many employees get pigeonholed, where the organization sees them as offering only one type of skill (such as accounting) when, in fact, the employees usually have broader talents to contribute. Share with employees the struggles of the organization and ask them what they have to contribute. What can they do to add value to the organization? You may be surprised what a wealth of ideas are trapped inside job descriptions. For example, at Johnsonville Foods a clerk in the accounting department, who suggested a new product line of catalog sales, ended up running the new division.

5. Employee's Personal Needs Are Not a Good Fit with the Organization or Job

Even if you involve employees in goal setting and provide them with career development services, some will still want and need to go in a different direction. Our first suggestion involves screening applicants for a good fit, but this is often not enough. As employees' needs change, the organization must improvise.

Employee's personal needs are not a good fit with the organization or job

- Use corporate image as a screening tool.
- Reassign the employee to a more appropriate position.
- Offer the employee a personal leave or sabbatical.
- Spin out the employee's venture.
- Offer outplacement assistance.

Use the Corporate Image as a Screening Tool

The alignment of employee and organizational needs is often best handled before the employee is hired. Organizations need to change so rapidly and they require employees who are willing to do new things.

One increasingly popular approach is to advertise the company image, not specific jobs. Instead of placing a classified ad for an operator, trainer, or secretary, these organizations place classified advertisements that discuss what it's like to work there and what attributes they seek in employees. In this way, potential applicants often screen themselves out of the process. Those who contact the organization in response to the ad can then be further educated and screened during the interview process. An added benefit of this approach is that it encourages employees to view a specific position as temporary. Employees hire on to the organization, not to a specific job.

Reassign an Employee to a More Appropriate Position

Over the years, employee needs and motivation will change—sometimes for good and sometimes only temporarily. Often these employees do not have to leave the organization. Instead, they can change jobs. For example, an employee with an injury or a new baby may need a less physically demanding job or less travel. Reassignment is often the best way to keep a valued employee.

In some organizations, employees are encouraged to take the initiative for proposing these changes. At Sequent Computer Systems, for example, employees are expected to develop a business case for pursuing new interests rather than to wait for the organization to make these decisions for them.[1] (See the section on inappropriate match of employee to job in Chapter Twelve.)

Offer the Employee a Personal Leave or Sabbatical

Sometimes a change in motivation or need is only temporary. Perhaps an employee needs time to adjust to changes in his or her personal life (a birth or family illness) or simply to recover from job burnout. Consider a temporary separation to maintain your investment in the employee.

Sabbaticals are also good opportunities to explore new interests, learn new skills, or rejuvenate energy. For example, as part of a massive restructuring effort, NYNEX allowed workers to take a two-year sabbatical for education, health, or other reasons. It even offered a $10,000 stipend for tuition.[2] Several high-tech firms also offer employees six-month sabbaticals every six or seven years. Make the most of this experience by helping the employee plan the time away and discuss both of your expectations about the results.

---

1. M.G. Brown; D. Hitchcock; and M. Willard, *Why TQM Fails and What to Do About It* (Chicago: Irwin Professional Publishing, 1994), p. 227.
2. C. Greer, "We Can Save Jobs," *Parade Magazine*, May 21, 1995, pp. 4–5.

Spin Out the Employee's Venture

 As organizations become more networked and entrepreneurial, it is increasingly likely that certain individuals will want to run their own show or have an idea that goes beyond the organization's mission. One option is to help launch the venture. This is especially attractive if the new venture is strategically tied to your business. Help employees build a business case for their ideas that includes the calculated return for the organization's investment. See *Intrapreneuring* by Gifford Pinchot III, and *When Giants Learn to Dance* by Rosabeth Moss Kanter.

Offer Outplacement Assistance

 As a last resort, the employee and organization go their separate ways. In these situations, organizations are wise to offer outplacement and retraining assistance. Your human resources department may be able to suggest good local resources. State employment agencies and community colleges are also a good place to begin; also look for outplacement consultants in your local phone directory.

Former employees who were helped to find their passion are more likely to speak kindly of their previous employer and purchase their services/products. In this competitive world, you can use all the advocates you can get!

14 Knowledge and Skills

People don't know how to do it right.

When confronted with an employee's mistake, many supervisors claim in exasperation, But I told him how to do it! The obvious response to a skill deficiency is to offer training. But this view is simplistic. First, you should make sure that a skill deficiency caused the mistake. Trainers often talk about the "Smith and Wesson test": If you put a gun to his head, could the employee do it? If the answer is yes, then you do *not* have a training problem. Instead you have either a motivational problem (the employee doesn't want to do it; see Chapter 13 for more on motivation) or an environmental obstacle (something is preventing the employee from doing it; see Part III for a discussion of structure and systems). Make sure you understand the illness before you prescribe the treatment!

Once you are sure the problem is a legitimate skill deficiency, you must identify the best way to impart the knowledge. Training is often helpful, but in certain circumstances it's a waste of time and money. If a task if performed infrequently, for example, a job aid (such as a checklist or process diagram) is often more appropriate.

In addition to considering the task that must be learned, you must also take into account the learner. Many factors may impact an individual's ability to learn and apply new skills. People differ in their preferred learning styles, so what helps one person may be of little value to someone else.

Review the symptoms that follow and determine the most likely cause of your people problem. Then turn to the cause to identify the appropriate treatment.

Symptoms

Employees don't want to learn the task. (5, 12,2, 12,3)

Employees are having trouble learning the task. (2, 3, 4, 5)

Employees are doing the task incorrectly most of the time. (1, 2, 12,2)

Employees have trouble remembering what to do when the time arises to do the task. (5)

Employees are having difficulty staying current in their field. (6)

The Peter Principle: Employees are promoted beyond their level of competence. (12,1)

Causes

1. Management isn't sure what skills employees need.

2. Employees don't know how to do the task.

3. Employees don't have an opportunity to practice the task.

4. The training method does not match the employee's learning style.

5. The content is hard to remember or learn.

6. Information and knowledge are changing so rapidly, it's hard to stay current.

(See also Chapter 12,1 "Inappropriate Match of Employee to the Job")

(See also Chapter 12,2 "Missing Basic Work Skills")

(See also Chapter 13,3 "Employees Can't See What's in It for Them.")

This cause may seem too obvious to mention, but in our experience, managers often delegate responsibilities without being clear about what the task is or what it takes to do it. This inevitably leads to problems.

This cause may also occur when an organization takes a new direction and no one in the organization has personal experience in the new environment. For example, the organization embarks on becoming a "high-performance organization," but no one in the organization has ever led such a transformation.

Two common approaches can clarify the skills needed to perform a task: conduct a task analysis or interview/observe experts.

Not sure what skills employees need

- Conduct a task analysis.
- Use expert interview and observation.

Conduct Task Analysis

A task analysis is appropriate when you are dealing with discrete tasks (such as interviewing job candidates, performing routine maintenance on a piece of equipment, or enrolling a customer in an IRA account) *and* the knowledge of how to perform the task exists in the organization.

There are numerous ways of performing task analyses. This simple approach will work in most instances:
- Assemble a representative sampling of people who know how to perform the task. These may include subject matter experts; people who designed the system, product, or service; those who perform the task regularly as well as their manager; those who teach the task; and perhaps even customers. (Using a group makes it less likely that you will omit important details.)

- List the steps necessary to perform the task. (This is when managers often realize they don't fully understand the task they are delegating.)

- For each step, describe anything that is difficult, tricky, or critical about performing the task. Also note any "tricks of the trade."

- For each step, list any knowledge, skills, or attitudes (KSAs) that are necessary to complete the task.

- Identify which KSAs the employees do not currently possess.

For more information, see *Figuring Things Out* by Zemke and Kramlinger. Also see "How Bell Labs Creates Star Performers" by Kelly and Caplan.

Use Expert Interview and Observation

If you need to determine the difference between mediocre and excellent performers, interviewing and observing experts will be more fruitful than relying on a task analysis. You can also use this method when those who have experience are outside your organization such as when you are beginning a new initiative.

Through observation and interviewing, you want to discover the beliefs, mental strategies, and behaviors that lead to success. You may learn what you need by just interviewing experts, but often it is insightful to compare their performance to that of average performers. By imitating the experts, employees should be able to close the gap between themselves and the experts. For more information, see *Unlimited Personal Power* by Anthony Robbins.

2. Employees Don't Know How to Do the Task

When faced with an employee who does not know how to perform a task, most managers instantly turn to training. However, there are several less expensive options that should be considered first.

Employees don't know how to do the task

- Simplify the task.
- Embed knowledge into the technology.
- Design a job aid.
- Provide training.

Simplify the Task

First, consider whether the task must be done at all or if there is a way to simplify the task so that it does not require special training. If you can't eliminate the task, you may be able to make the process obvious. For example, if employees are to put different products on different spindles, design the spindles in different shapes so that it's obvious which product goes where (i.e., the square peg in the square hole). Fast food cash registers are another example of making a task obvious. Instead of entering the value of the burger, the employee simply presses the burger button. Use conventions that are familiar to most people in the culture. For example, red, yellow, and green have familiar meanings in most industrialized countries. Design the task so it's hard to do wrong.

Embed the Knowledge into the Technology

Often the task is too complex to have an obvious solution. Instead, you must make it easy for workers to get access to the best information. You can embed formulas into electronic spreadsheets and use boilerplates for legal documents in word-processing packages. Grocery scanning systems provide the current prices. Focus on reducing the opportunity for error by developing well-tested programs to handle complex tasks or tedious data entry.

In most knowledge work, the trick is to get access to the experts' approaches—without having to bother the experts! Here again, technology is often the answer. Expert systems and artificial intelligence are currently guiding investment brokers, medical professionals, and oil drillers. Researchers are experimenting with "telemedicine," which may eventually enable a physician in one location to perform remote surgery on a patient at another site. With interactive videodisk, CD-ROM, performance support systems, the information superhighway, and other emerging technologies, providing employees with immediate feedback and advice should be easier than ever.

If you choose this option to help employees perform their jobs, be sure that they use the technology. For example, some stock brokerages have built expert systems to review a client's portfolio and recommend investments. However, many brokers resist using the system (at least in part) because they want the client to identify with them, not with the firm or the firm's computer system.

Design a Job Aid

Job aids are tools that help employees perform specific tasks. They are most helpful for tasks that employees do infrequently (such as periodic maintenance) or that must be performed precisely (such as a pilot's preflight check). Job aids include worksheets, checklists, diagrams, procedures, and manuals. Use the following chart to decide which aid might be best for your task.

Nature of Task	Job Aid
Inspecting, observing, planning.	Checklist
Step-by-step actions.	Procedure or flowchart
Simple decision making.	Decision table (This chart is an example of decision table.)
Complex decision making; multiple variables.	Decision flowchart (These are more complex than decision tables and usually have multiple branches.)
Documentation or computation.	Worksheet

Be sure to design the job aid with input from the employees who will use it and the experts who know how to do the task. Also, establish a regular schedule to review the job aid so that it stays current.

Provide Training

Training can be used in conjunction with all of the above options. Before you send an employee to a workshop, however, be sure you have answered these questions:

- What *exactly* does the employee need to know?

- Does this training workshop specifically address needs?

- How does the workshop verify that the employee has learned what he/she needs to know, and what remediation is available?

- How is the employee expected to use the new knowledge or skills on the job shortly after the workshop?

- How well is the employee expected to do it?

- What follow-up will the employee require to reinforce the learning?

If no formal workshop is available, you will need to provide on-the-job training. Follow these steps to prepare for a productive learning experience:

- List all of the steps necessary to complete the task.

- Identify anything that is difficult about performing the steps, or any "tricks of the trade."

- Outline what you will cover with the employee. In general, begin with a broad overview and then get into specifics.

- Use questions to guide the employee's learning.

- Plan ways to verify that the employee is learning; use questions, give case studies, simulate the task, etc. (See the next section for more information on practicing tasks.)

Provide the training close to the time when the employee will need to use the skills. Just-in-time training, while requiring extra effort, is far superior to its alternative, which has been described as "spray and pray."

3. Employees Don't Have an Opportunity to Practice the Task

Proficiency is gained only through practice. Employees must have frequent opportunities to practice their skills. Sometimes, the natural flow of work does not provide such opportunities, so they must be created. Here are several options to provide reinforcement and practice.

Employees don't have an opportunity to practice the task

- Create a special project that requires employees to use the skill.
- Provide performance feedback.
- Simulate the task.

Create a Special Project That Requires Employees to Use the Skill

Before employees attend training, they should have in mind specific opportunities that will require the use of the new skills. If the individual's job does not provide immediate opportunities to apply the skills, the manager can assign a special project that does require it. For example, an employee who attended project management or leadership training might be assigned to lead a quality-improvement team.

Provide Performance Feedback

Formal training is rarely sufficient to create proficiency. Usually the employee needs continued reinforcement and performance feedback on the job. Managers or other subject-matter experts should plan time to observe and give feedback to the employee, coaching them through the process while it is being performed. To make this process work, managers obviously need to be well versed in the content of the training and the work itself. Feedback should always be specific and timely and presented as soon as possible after the observation. (See Chapter 11 on rewards.)

Simulate the Task

Sometimes it is not possible to create an opportunity for the employee to perform the task "for real." Perhaps it is too risky (such as responding to a hazardous waste spill or nuclear meltdown) or the opportunities are infrequent (such as taking corrective action during a mechanical failure or stock market crash). In these cases, develop a simulation that tests the employee's proficiency and provides regular practice.

Simulations can be as simple as a staged role play or as elaborate as a sophisticated flight simulator. Computers offer an exciting array of simulations. Many off-the-shelf programs provide rich learning experiences in planning and decision making for teams or executives. Depending on the complexity of the simulation, some or all of the icons may apply. See the chapter on microworlds in Senge's *Fifth Discipline Fieldbook*. See also "Communities of Commitment: The Heart of Learning Organizations" by Kofman and Senge. To learn how to build your own simulation, see "Building Instructional Games" by Darcy Hitchcock.

4. The Training Method Does Not Match the Employee's Learning Style

While we all take in information through our five senses, each person learns differently. Make sure you adjust your teaching strategies to the employee's preferred learning styles.

The training method does not match the employee's learning style

- Conduct a learning-styles assessment.
- Provide for multiple learning styles.
- Use accelerated learning techniques.

Conduct a Learning-Styles Assessment

If you are training one person or a small number of individuals over time, it may be useful to administer a learning-styles assessment. Or you can simply ask the individuals how they prefer to learn. Have them place the following learning strategies in the preferred order, omitting any they do not favor:

• Read about it.

• Experience it.

• Do it with feedback.

• Give it a try on my own.

• Tell me about it.

• Show me pictures/visuals/diagrams.

• Give me an overview of it.

• Explain it in detail.

• Observe someone doing it.

• Talk about it with others.

Once you know the preferred styles of your students, you can adjust your training approach.

Provide for Multiple Learning Styles

If you have more than one learner, you're likely to be faced with multiple learning styles. If you can't treat each person individually, your best option is to use a variety of teaching methods that address all three predominant learning styles. Use visuals as you discuss the task. Demonstrate the task while letting some students participate. Devise learning activities that provide opportunities to practice (such as simulations, role plays, case studies, and actual job tasks.). See "Different Strokes: Learning Styles in the Classroom" by Bob Filipczak.

Use Accelerated-Learning Techniques

Accelerated-learning techniques force the integrated use of all parts of the brain. Traditional training strategies (i.e., lecture, reading, rote practice) are directed only at the mental process that resides largely in the brain's left hemisphere. Research indicates that learning and retention are greatly enhanced if instruction can systematically address both hemispheres while taking into account our emotional and physical states.

Consider incorporating some of these accelerated-learning strategies into your training.

Left brain/right brain strategies
• Use mental practice and imagery.

• Use mind maps, structured texts, and advance organizers to help workers anticipate and organize the learning.

- Include a constant mix of visual, auditory, and kinesthetic (physical) approaches.

- Review material frequently and in a variety of ways.

- Create connections between what the learner may already know and what is being taught.

- Change approaches every 10 minutes where possible (e.g., move from a flip chart/interactive lecture to a small-group activity).

Psychological strategies
- Elicit a reason to learn the material.

- Create a relaxed and trusting atmosphere.

- Support the learner's self-esteem.

- Provide corrective but tactful feedback.

- Minimize competition among learners.

Physical strategies
- Eliminate distractions from the environment.

- Provide a comfortable space (adequate lighting, functional furniture, comfortable room temperature).

- Arrange furniture to maximize interaction.

- Break every 60 minutes.

For a quick lesson on how to design training sessions, see the series of articles called "Talking Ain't Teaching" by Joel Gendelman.

5. The Content Is Hard to Remember or Learn

Sometimes the content is just hard to learn or remember. This is often the case with detailed information. Here are several strategies to facilitate learning.

The content is hard to remember or learn

- Create a job aid.
- Develop a mnemonic or acronym.
- Develop an instructional game.
- Provide "fluency" training.

Create a Job Aid

The best training option may be not to try to make people remember how to do a job. If employees have access to a job aid as a resource, they may only need to learn how to use the aid.

Job aids are tools that help employees perform specific tasks. They are most helpful for tasks that employees do infrequently (such as periodic maintenance) or that must be performed precisely (such as a pilot's preflight check). Job aids include worksheets, checklists, diagrams, procedures, and manuals. Use the following chart to decide which aid might be best for your task.

Nature of Task	Job Aid
Inspecting, observing, planning.	Checklist
Step-by-step actions.	Procedure or flowchart
Simple decision making.	Decision table (This chart is an example of decision table.)
Complex decision making; multiple variables.	Decision flowchart (These are more complex than decision tables and usually have multiple branches.)
Documentation or computation.	Worksheet

Be sure to design the job aid with input from the employees who will use it and the experts who know how to do the task. Also, establish a regular schedule to review the job aid so that it stays current.

Develop a Mnemonic or Acronym

If the task does not allow employees to use a job aid (for example, if their hands are not free or time does not allow for looking something up), then a memory aid can help. Many of us remember the number of days in each month and whether *E* comes before *I* with a rhyme. Mnemonics and acronyms are also helpful. (FACE are the spaces between the lines in music; Every Good Boy Does Fine are the lines.) Ideally, the memory aid should reinforce the content. For example, one of the authors once created FAIR as the acronym to help managers remember the four criteria for avoiding equal-opportunity problems, fairness being the main concern:[1]

Factors are objective—not subjective.

Administered uniformly—the policy is the same for all people in a job classification.

Impact is consistent—the decision has no adverse effect on people in protected classes.

Related to the job.

---

1. From the "On the Line" training program. Copyright 1986 Pacific Learning Systems.

Develop an Instructional Game

When the content is dry, a creative learning activity can make it more fun to learn. Board games, card games, TV game shows, video games, and complex simulations are all possible models. The steps for creating a game are to:

- Analyze the task to identify learning objectives and necessary game attributes.

- Examine known games to use as a model.

- Define the game components (board? dice? cards?).

- Develop a prototype of the game.

- Test and revise the game.

For more information, see "Building Instructional Games" by Darcy Hitchcock.

Provide Fluency Training

Can you remember your first telephone number? Many people can't, although they knew it by heart at one point. "Fluency" training techniques make learning extremely resistant to being forgotten. This training approach uses high-speed practice (as with flash cards) to cement the material into the learners' memories. This model is ideally suited to situations where immediate and complete recall of key knowledge is essential for performance.

6. Information and Knowledge Are Changing So Rapidly, It's Hard to Stay Current

In some fields, the problem is not so much learning the content but rather unlearning and relearning fast enough. Medical research, computer technology, and space exploration are creating information so fast that it's hard to keep up. New laws and new court rulings are passed every day. Yesterday's truth becomes today's falsehood. How can you keep up? We have several suggestions.

Information and knowledge are changing so rapidly, it's hard to stay current

- Assign various learning responsibilities to different people on the team.
- Centralize the information.
- Centralize the function.
- Outsource the work.

Assign Various Learning Responsibilities to Different People on the Team

In this information age, it's easy to become overwhelmed. One way to handle the information overload is to share the responsibility. Identify the learning areas critical to your work and assign one to each person on your team. Perhaps one person can monitor new EPA rulings while another stays in touch with OSHA. Then develop ways to identify when information should be shared. See Chapter 15 for more ideas.

Centralize the Information

One problem with rapidly changing information is that it's hard to ensure that everyone has accurate and current data. One solution is to centralize the information (or create a distributed network). Everyone has access to the same information at the same time, and the information needs to be updated in only one location. The New York Stock Exchange and airlines reservation systems are examples of centralized information systems. In addition, many distribution centers are uploading sales data to centralized databases and downloading data from their customer's inventory systems so everyone in the organization can use the same information. See various articles in *Forbes ASAP* Supplements for examples.

One emerging technology is groupware that allows people who are geographically dispersed to work together. The term is used to describe everything from e-mail to concurrent engi-neering systems. See "A Skeptic's Guide to Groupware" by Glenn Rifkin for an overview of the management issues involved in implementing groupware systems.

Centralize the Function

Another option, which was perhaps more popular in the past, is to centralize the function. In effect, the job of one person or department is to stay up-to-date. This centralized resource reviews all relevant decisions before they are finalized. Corporate attorneys, for example, often review contracts before they are signed. Beware: This person or department can become a bottleneck, reducing the flexibility and responsiveness of the organization. Also, where knowledge equals power, this approach can create fiefdoms rapidly.

Outsource the Work

One way to centralize the function is to outsource the work, hiring the best organization in the field that you can afford. Bottlenecks are still a potential drawback but often the competitive customer/supplier relationship improves performance over in-house resources. Be sure to manage the relationship carefully so that a close partnership emerges. See "Innovators in Outsourcing" by Howard Anderson, *Break-Through Partnering: Creating a Collective Enterprise Advantage* by Patricia Moody, and *Making Organizations Competitive: Enhancing Networks and Relationships across Traditional Boundaries* by Ralph and Ines Kilmann.

One risk with this strategy is that you may outsource something that will become a critical competency later. For example, when IBM designed the personal computer, it apparently decided that its core competencies were marketing and distribution and outsourced the operating system and the chip. History shows that IBM guessed wrong. Microsoft and Intel have thrived while IBM languished. See *The End of Bureaucracy and the Rise of the Intelligent Organization* by Gifford Pinchot.

15 Shared Learning

We are missing opportunities because we don't know how to leverage and act on our shared learning.

Many of the concepts we have talked about in previous chapters (empowerment, total quality, reengineering, etc.) are all powerful tools for achieving high performance. Maintaining high-performing, healthy organizations, however, requires a commitment to continuous learning. You would no sooner go to a doctor who had ceased to read the medical journals than you would invest in an organization that does not support learning, risk taking, and innovation. Sadly, though, few organizations have the understanding or the infrastructures necessary to promote learning. Review the problems listed below to help you identify your own organization's obstacles to learning.

Symptoms	Causes
Every business unit operates differently. (4, 5)	1. Employees don't have good group-learning skills.
We keep reinventing the wheel. (4, 5)	2. Employees don't know how to capture their learning.
We are slow to create and act on innovative ideas. (1, 2, 3)	3. Employees don't know how to apply what they learn.
We can't seem to leverage the ideas and intelligence of our workforce. (1, 2, 3)	4. We do not have a forum for sharing what we learn.
We are not open to new ideas. (5)	5. People have trouble learning from others with different views.
If it wasn't "invented here," we don't want it. (5)	

R̸X

1. Employees Don't Have Good Group-Learning Skills

In 1988 the Department of Labor co-published with the American Society for Training and Development a report that summarizes the workplace skills most required by employers. The top of the list and cornerstone for all the others was knowing how to learn. Because information is so quickly outdated, people are no longer hired for what they know so much as for what they can learn. Group learning—learning that is shared and leads to collective action—is critical to maintaining high-performance efforts. Consider some of the following strategies for promoting group learning.

Employees don't have good group-learning skills

- Establish ground rules for learning.
- Approach every situation as a learning opportunity.
- Allow time for reflection.

Establish Ground Rules for Learning

Establishing group-learning ground rules is a good first step toward fostering learning. They will not only facilitate the learning process but also will force attention to the issue of learning. You may choose to incorporate your learning rules into your existing set of meeting ground rules. If you believe that group learning is very alien to your work unit, they may get more attention if they are documented and posted separately.

Begin the development of your rules list with a thought-provoking question such as, What makes it hard for us to share information and insights? See if you can draft a list of rules that will prevent or mitigate those obstacles. If your group has trouble identifying the obstacles, consider some of these issues:

- Are people unlikely to share information because doing so will erode their power or influence?

- Are people comfortable admitting when they don't understand something?

- Is information readily accessible?

- Are people blamed for their failures, or are people encouraged to share their failures and use them as learning opportunities?

- Are people able to give direct and honest feedback, or are they likely to say only what they think others want to hear?

- Do people tiptoe around some "undiscussable" topics?

- Do we use information to place blame?

Approach Every Situation as a Learning Opportunity

Our "learning paradigm" often blinds us to the most important learning opportunities. The traditional model for learning is a passive, episodic event where someone (an expert) pours information into our heads. In reality that is seldom how real learning occurs. Real learning results when we encounter situations that are novel or that require a skill or understanding that we recognize we don't have. When viewed in this light, it is quite likely that groups face learning opportunities dozens of times a week: whenever there is conflict among team members, whenever a group is faced with a problem, whenever a group wants to create something new or establish a new relationship either within or outside the team. Teach your group to ask two questions after any exchange: What can we (or did we) learn from this situation? What does this situation imply we should do differently in the future? For more ideas see Chris Argyris's article "Teaching Smart People How to Learn," and the McCall, Lombardo, and Morrison article "How Successful Executives Develop on the Job."

Allow Time for Reflection

In the United States our cultural biases against reflection inhibit our ability to learn. We equate reflection with "day dreaming" or "goofing off." We are really working only when we are visibly doing something. But, unless group members are given the opportunity to reflect on data, the perspectives of others, or their own processes, no true learning can occur.

Try some of these strategies for structuring the skill or habit of reflection into your group processes:

- Journals—Ask each person in your group to keep a personal journal. You may choose to focus the content (list specific work problems, record your thoughts about the last team meeting, document the results of certain actions) or leave it wide open. Until the habit is established, encourage everyone to make regular entries (daily, weekly, etc.). People are often surprised at what they write and frequently learn new things about themselves.

- Delay decisions—Our action orientation often causes us to rush decisions before an issue receives sufficient thought. Try postponing group decisions until the next meeting to purposely give people time to reflect on the issue.

- Change the subject—When a problem becomes too muddled or divisive, try tabling the issue and going on to something else. The most creative thoughts often arise when we consciously let go of a problem for a while.

- Call for silence—When conversation isn't getting anywhere, call for a period of silence. Agree beforehand how long the silence should last and get everyone's commitment to hold to it. To get the full benefit of this forced reflection, make sure that it lasts at least five minutes. It generally takes a few minutes to clear our minds and turn off the internal conversation.

Humans are driven to learn continuously, but the benefits of this learning to the group or organization are lost unless that learning is somehow captured and acted upon. The strategies listed here will help build the discipline for documenting and sharing learning among teams and work groups.

Employees don't know how to capture their learning

- Keep a learning log.
- Conduct team-improvement reviews.

Keep a Learning Log

As described in Chapter 10 feedback is an invaluable learning resource. Few work groups, however, take advantage of this resource to leverage their group learning. A learning log is a simple tool that helps work groups organize, process, and track data for the purpose of learning. The log may be an electronic database or a simple three-ring binder. The content of the log will be specific to the needs of the group, but consider the following as potential content sections:

• Meeting notes or decision logs.

• Graphs of performance measures.

• An idea bank.

• Research reports.

• Bibliographies or resource directories.

• Lists of improvement goals and their associated action plans.

• Benchmark data.

Conduct Team-Improvement Reviews

Team-improvement reviews are regularly scheduled planning and problem-solving meetings. Getting into the habit of periodically reviewing your progress builds a discipline for learning. Logical times for conducting improvement reviews are at major milestones in your group's process: at the end of a project, at your annual business-planning session, at the end of a season. These reviews follow a simple outline.

1. The group reviews past performance. The learning log should provide good data for this discussion, as should the feedback of group members and customers.

2. The group "problem solves" around any unsatisfactory results. What was the cause of these results? What can the group learn from this information? What does this information imply for the future?

3. The group documents learnings and sets both new output and learning goals for the next period. All of this information should be included in the learning log to ensure that none of the learnings or decisions are lost.

For more information about team-improvement reviews, see Chapter 9 in *Why Teams Can Fail and What to Do about It* by Hitchcock and Willard.

3. Employees Don't Know How to Apply What They Learn

Learning and application are powerful partners. Like the chicken and the egg, it is difficult to say which is the cause of which. We know, however, that the real benefit of group learning is realized when employees apply that learning and achieve tangible results. The previous sections described strategies for assuring that learning takes place. This section presents strategies for assuring that learning gets translated into meaningful actions.

Employees don't know how to apply what they learn

- Make learning problem centered.
- Use simulations or microworlds.
- Commit publicly to ideas.
- Measure learning.

Make Learning Problem Centered

Research indicates that adults both retain and apply more of what they learn when they can relate that learning to some current problem. Use this information to maximize learning in your own group. When designing or selecting training, for example, make sure that the training relates directly to the current issues of your group. It should explicitly describe how to apply what is learned to their problem as well as give participants the opportunity to test their new skills or knowledge on the problem during the training. This learning principle applies even in informal settings. As explained earlier, turn every problem-solving session into a learning session by taking the time to talk about and document what was learned in the process and how your new learnings could be applied elsewhere.

Use Simulations or Microworlds

An effective strategy for increasing the likelihood that new learnings are used is to create a learning environment that replicates the actual work environment as much as possible. Simulating a performance situation allows a learner to experiment safely with new ideas and practice new skills. Role-play exercises—a form of simulation—allow learners to simulate conversations with others. Computer technology now allows for more complex and realistic simulations through applications called "microworlds." Microworlds provide practice fields for teams and managers for such skills as creating visions, testing decisions, integrating ideas, and testing mental models. Having this opportunity to try out new skills, especially in a collaborative format, is critical to establishing both the competence and confidence learners need to generalize learning to new situations. For more information on microworlds, see Peter Senge's book *The Fifth Discipline* and Chapter 14 of this book.

Commit Publicly to Ideas

Sometimes learning doesn't get applied because the employees lack the commitment or confidence to try out their new skills or ideas. Going public with your ideas and intentions often provides the impetus to follow through. The team-improvement review (as described above) provides a good opportunity for publicly committing to action within the team. Committing outside the team involves more risk but also tends to increase the commitment. It also provides the opportunity to involve more people in the idea, which in itself tends to increase the chance of follow-through.

Measure Learning

All of the strategies mentioned so far move away from the casual approach to learning that organizations traditionally take. This last strategy, measuring learning outcomes, formalizes the learning process, more than all the others. Several reasons for explicitly measuring learning follow:
• To clarify what is expected of the learners.

- To focus attention on the critical aspects of the learning process.

- To lend emphasis. (People tend to pay attention if they know they will be measured.)

- To provide a means for assessing the value of the experience. Was it worth the time and money invested in it?

To enhance the application of new skills, focus the measures on what people should be able to do as a result of new learnings as well as a minimum standard for how well they should be able to do it. (See the following example.) Involve the learners in the collection and analysis of these results so that they get immediate feedback on their learning and the value of the experience.

Instead of . . .	Try . . .
Complete eight hours of telephone sales training.	1. Identify the customer's need within the first 30 seconds of a call.
	2. Summarize expectations of both you and the customer and get the customer's acknowledgment.
	3. Never close a call with a customer without assuring that the customer's need has been met.

4. We Do Not Have a Forum for Sharing What We Learn

Similar to the issue of applying learning is the issue of sharing learning. Few organizations have the infrastructures to support the exchange of information or new learnings. Consider some of the following strategies for institutionalizing learning exchanges.

We do not have a forum for sharing what we learn

- Host a learning event.
- Build matrixed/linked structures.
- Create accessible information systems.

Host a Learning Event

A learning event can take many forms. You can build a learning event around a system audit, a quality fair, a search conference, or a resource expo. There are several advantages to this approach. A major event is a good way to get the attention of the members of your organization. Expending considerable time and energy will demonstrate the organization's value for learning more than any amount of rhetoric. Learning events also provide an opportunity for all members of an organization to mingle across their functional boundaries or independent work units and to share experiences and information. Last, they provide an opportunity for people to apply or at least demonstrate what they have learned. This level of involvement not only reinforces learning (we learn best that which we know we will have to teach) but also requires a public commitment to share learning (see "Commit Publicly" in the previous section as well as Chapter 9 for more information). For other examples see "High-Impact Learning: Building and Diffusing Learning Capability" by Ulrich, Jick, and Von Glinow.

Build Matrixed/Linked Structures

The down side to learning events is that they are sporadic as opposed to continuous. Learning has the chance of falling off between events. Another strategy is to create a permanent infrastructure that ensures continuous sharing. Matrixing or linking different groups together increases the likelihood that information and learning will be shared. One familiar method is the "star point" or "peer sphere" structure that defines common roles among work groups and then creates teams out of these common roles. Matrix management, cross-functional problem solving, or quality-improvement committees, are other strategies that encourage cross-pollination. Other organizations achieve shared learning by rotating staff through various positions or work groups. New team members bring to their new roles the learnings from past experiences, thereby seeding ideas throughout the organization. For more information see "Linking Arrangements and New Work Designs" by Kolodny and Dresner. Whatever your strategy, consider a structure that crosses many boundaries: vertical (up and down the hierarchy); horizontal (across functional or product groups); external (involving customers, suppliers, even competitors); and geographic.

Create Accessible Information Systems

Before it can be used, information must be accessible. The two biggest obstacles to accessibility are ineffective storage practices and data protection policies. For some organizations the information exists in abundance, but no one knows where it is or how to find it. Needed information may be scattered throughout the organization or tucked away in dusty closets. Potential users are further deterred by unnavigable cataloging systems. In other cases the enemy to shared information is the protectionist policies that bar all but those with proper clearance from accessing data. Any policy that limits the free flow of information effectively undermines the potential for your organization to become a learning organization.

We are fortunate to have the technology to allow effortless information sharing. Creative companies make use of the ability to create linked databases of information to not only facilitate browsing but also to prompt users to check related information in other parts of the system. Electronic libraries of like projects, best practices, structured references, and research data put employees in immediate touch with a plethora of usable data. The technology further assists by facilitating the collection, manipulation, and transmittal of information throughout the organization and even around the world. Groupware software programs facilitate the exchange of information among team members and their stakeholders. Organizations that don't leverage this technology will be woefully handicapped in their ability to learn and keep pace.

The Virtual Corporation by Davidow and Malone is a good reference on using information technology to build flexible organizations.

You can lead a horse to water but you can't make it drink. Creating opportunities for people to come together and share ideas does not guarantee that learning will occur. Unless we are open to what we are hearing, we are unlikely to absorb and retain what is being presented. Many patients miss out on potentially valuable treatments because of their cultural biases against alternative practices such as homeopathy and acupuncture. The following strategies can help people break down the barriers and prejudices that get in the way of creating a learning organization.

People have trouble learning from others with different views

- Teach good listening skills.
- Practice dialogue.
- Benchmark best practices.

Teach Good Listening Skills

There are so many things that work against our ability to listen, not the least of which is a dearth of good listening skills. Share and then demonstrate the following listening techniques with your own group:

- Stop talking—Though obvious it seems hard to remember. You can't listen and talk at the same time.

- Imagine the other person's point of view—Try to walk in her or his shoes if only for a moment.

- Look and act interested—Make eye contact; nod.

- Watch nonverbal cues—You can "hear" a lot from a person's expression and body language.

- Don't interrupt—Fight the urge to respond.

- Stick to constructive replies—Resist the temptation to formulate your rebuttal at least until you have acknowledged the speaker.

- Paraphrase—Recapping the main points not only convinces the other person you were listening but also reinforces your own learning of what you heard.

For more on good listening skills, see Rick Ross's piece called "Skillful Discussions" in Peter Senge's *The Fifth Discipline Fieldbook*.

Practice Dialogue

Dialogue is a useful group-learning tool. Dialogue differs from discussion in that no attempt is made to convince or sell. In a dialogue participants agree to share ideas or views while suspending all judgment. The purpose of a dialogue is not to chose among the presented ideas but to create something totally new using all the ideas. Follow these steps to begin a dialogue with your group.

- Agree on the ground rules for a dialogue: give everyone a chance to speak uninterrupted and treat all ideas as valid and valuable.

- Once all the ideas or positions have been expressed, invite the group to design as many possibilities or inventions that include as many of the ideas as possible.

- Debrief the dialogue using the following questions: What did we learn? What insights or new possibilities have we discovered? Are any of these new possibilities worth pursuing further?

To assure success, it is important that the participants have good dialoguing skills. These skills include the following abilities:

- Provide others with accurate, complete, and relevant information.

- Acknowledge the competence of other participants even when disagreeing with them.

- Make apparent the reasoning behind a position.

- Describe the line of thinking that led to a conclusion.

- Voice the point of view of others.

- Willingly change position in the face of convincing data.

- Regard assertions as hypotheses to test.

- Challenge errors in others' reasoning.[1]

For more information on dialogue, see the articles by William Isaacs "Taking Flight: Dialogue, Collective Thinking, and Organizational Learning," and Edgar Schein "On Dialogue, Culture and Organizational Learning."

Benchmark Best Practices

 Benchmarking helps companies identify improvement opportunities by comparing their processes and products to those of others. It is a disciplined process that requires significant investments in time and resources to search out best practices. Benchmarking without an open mind is the equivalent of industrial tourism. Benchmarking can be conducted internally, comparing the processes and outputs of various parts of an organization, or externally against competitors. World-class benchmarking involves identifying organizations that may be outside your own industry who are the best at certain processes or products. The biggest leaps in innovations tend to come from this last type of benchmarking. Progressive hospitals, for example, are benchmarking hotels for best practices in admitting. What hospitals frequently take hours to do with patients, hotels do in minutes with guests.

For more information on benchmarking, see one of the following resources: *Benchmarking: The Search for Industry Best Practices That Lead to Superior Performance* by Robert Camp, *Improving through Benchmarking: A Practical Guide* by Richard Chang, or *The Benchmarking Book* by Michael Spendolini.

---

1. N. Dixon, "A Practical Model for "Organizational Learning," *Issues & Observations*, 15, no. 2 (1995), pp. 1–4.

PART V OUTSIDE INFLUENCES

The source of an organizational illness is not always inside. Sometimes "bugs" come in the form of troublesome regulations that may need to be changed, and problems may stem from involuntary alliances, such as restrictive labor contracts or meddlesome parent companies. Voluntary alliances, such as with customers and suppliers, often seem easier to solve than involuntary ones because you can walk away from the relationship. However, usually that action is a Band-Aid. To survive in the next century, we will need to operate in increasingly trusting and collaborative relationships across organizational boundaries. So walking away is rarely a viable prescription.

Environmental changes can affect an organization's health (e.g., new competition, changes in your labor market, or a technological breakthrough that makes your product or service obsolete). Sometimes the environment has changed so radically that death is likely unless you are able to adapt. In Part V, we address the external factors that can inhibit the health and viability of your organization.

Regulations	Regulations inhibit us from doing the right things.	Chapter 16
Involuntary alliances	Critical stakeholders will not allow us to do what we need to be successful.	Chapter 17
Voluntary alliances	Our "partners" are inhibiting our progress.	Chapter 18
Global trends	The future does not bode well for us.	Chapter 19

16 Regulations

Regulations inhibit us from doing the right things.

Almost every organization is constrained to some extent by contractual obligations, government regulations, or both. Many would liken these obligations to being in traction—tied to a hospital bed and with limited mobility. However, these regulations and legal clauses are established to benefit us all. No one wants to return to the days when the Cuyahoga River in Cleveland was so polluted it burned or when blood donations to the Red Cross were not screened for AIDS. Would you want to buy a house that was built without any construction codes? Would you buy shares on the stock exchanges if insider trading were permitted?

However, regulations and certain contractual obligations can also cause inequities and inefficiencies. Some are patently outdated and no longer serve a purpose. Organizations must be able to identify those obligations that are no longer in the best interest of our society and work to eliminate them. They must also be able to accept those that are in the best interest of our community and learn to work effectively within them. The first step, however, is to ask, Are we really prevented from doing what we need to? Often the mysterious "they" (who won't let us do something) don't exist. Never use regulations as an excuse to stop improving.

Review the following list of symptoms to help you identify the underlying causes of your problems; then refer to the appropriate section.

Symptoms

We perceive regulations to be preventing us from achieving our goals. (1, 2)

We don't have the energy/resources to "buck the system." (1, 5)

We disagree with the value of some of the regulations. (2, 3, 4, 5)

Causes

1. The regulation is being used as an excuse for not making changes.

2. The regulation is in the best interest of the society but not the organization.

3. The regulation was created to resolve past abuses.

4. The regulations contradict each other.

5. The regulations provide no incentive to improve.

1. The Regulation Is Being Used as an Excuse for Not Making Changes

Because regulations and contracts are imposed by outside forces, it is all too easy for organizations to use them as excuses for their problems. Life somehow seems easier when there is a scapegoat for our problems. In reality, though, if we don't accept some responsibility for our woes, we will be impotent to do anything about them. Recent medical evidence indicates that patients who take control of their own conditions fare much better, even against the most serious illnesses, than those who blame science for their failure to get well.

The regulation is being used as an excuse for not making changes

- Study the regulation.
- Identify the common ground.
- Clarify the latitude allowed.

Study the Regulation

Begin by doing your homework. Don't base your beliefs on assumptions about the intent and letter of the regulation or contract. Sometimes just studying the regulation will clear up misconceptions and alert people to the lameness of their excuse. To get the best understanding of the regulation or contract terms, review information from several resources. The actual document is the place to start. Review it for understanding. If you need help with interpretation, seek counsel from a variety of sources. The issuing government agency or union will provide one perspective. You may also need to seek legal counsel or technical consulting services to get another perspective. Be sure that your research at least provides you answers to the following questions:

Purpose: What is the intent of this regulation/contractual clause? What need is it designed to fulfill or what problem was it designed to solve?

Players: Who are the key stakeholders of this regulation? Whose needs was it designed to address?

Proof: What data was used to justify the regulation? Is that data still accurate and relevant? Is there now existing data that is different?

Identify the Common Ground

Assuming you have a good understanding of the intent of the regulation or contract, compare that to the intent and the values of your own organization. Where is there overlap or common ground? While there may be places where your values differ, focus on those areas where you are in agreement. The common ground gives you a point from which to negotiate and to begin generating creative alternatives that meet everyone's needs. Many regulations, for example, are designed to prevent organizations from damaging the environment. Few companies find this intent to be in conflict with their own values, but often the prescribed requirements are difficult to fulfill. One enterprising steel mill eliminated the need to follow an elaborate and expensive disposal process for one of its toxic waste products by finding another manufacturing process that used the waste as its raw material—turning a headache into a profit without violating the regulation.

Clarify the Latitude Allowed

If you can convince all the key stakeholders of your common interests, you can more successfully explore the regulation with them to determine the amount of latitude it permits for alternative solutions. Sometimes it is not the letter of the law that prevents an organization from trying new approaches, but the lack of trust that has developed among the stakeholders. One county government agency, for example, was able to greatly revise certain of its job descriptions without rewriting either its contract with the union or the government job-classification system within which it operates. It did work very hard at building solid and trusting relationships with both the union and the personnel office so that everyone could agree on the level of latitude and discretion allowed within the existing language.

2. The Regulation Is in the Best Interest of the Society but Not the Organization

Sometimes the regulations or legal obligations an organization must deal with are in the best interests of the community but not in the best interests of the organization. No one could feel justified in demanding priority attention in an emergency room for a broken leg while someone else is having a heart attack. Still it's hard to sit and wait with a broken leg. However, honoring those rules that serve the greater good does not necessarily mean sitting powerlessly and suffering. Consider some of the strategies presented here to mitigate your discomfort.

The regulation is in the best interest of the society but not the organization.

- Develop creative ways to mitigate the negative effect of the regulation on the organization.

- Develop marketable expertise around the regulation.

- Participate in the shaping of the regulation.

Develop Creative Ways to Mitigate the Negative Effect of the Regulation on the Organization

Few organizations want to be an instrument of harm to their communities. Frequently, however, the regulations and obligations add expense and inconvenience to many businesses. This situation isn't sufficient excuse to violate the law. It is, however, an opportunity to reexamine processes and invent improvements. As an example, many states have instituted "bottle bills" that require beverage bottles to carry a 5- to 10-cent deposit to discourage littering. The burden to collect both the deposit and the returning bottles falls to grocery stores and requires additional staff and storage space. One major grocery chain took the law as a challenge to improve customer service. It is experimenting with "reverse" vending machines outside of the stores that accept pop cans and dispense redeemable vouchers. Customers can return cans day or night without waiting for a clerk. This innovative system also lessens demands on staff time as well as storage space.

Develop Marketable Expertise around the Regulation

Another strategy for dealing with restrictive regulations is to turn the inconvenience into profit. If being knowledgeable about a particular law or regulation is of value to the organization anyway, why not take the time to develop the expertise and then sell your knowledge to others in your business. CH2M HILL, LTD, a 50-year-old environmental engineering and consulting services firm, became so knowledgeable about water pollution control and the delivery of services that it began to sell operations and maintenance services to municipal water- and waste-treatment customers. It has spun off a separate business called Operations Management International (OMI) that contracts to operate and maintain municipal utility services as well as to support its companion companies in delivering a total package of services to these customers.

Participate in the Shaping of the Regulation

Certainly it is in an organization's best interests to be involved in the shaping of any regulation or contract that impacts its business. While it would be unconscionable to suggest any strategy that undermines an attempt to protect society or contributes to a situation of conflict of interest, decisions regarding regulations are best made with information from all sides of the issue. Auto manufacturers, for example, were instrumental in helping legislators craft workable emissions control laws. Similarly, most electronics and telecommunications firms participate in establishing the standards and regulations that govern their emerging businesses. Savvy organizations are learning the benefits of taking a proactive approach to negotiating union contracts by sharing financial information so that realistic contract terms can be established.

If you are not already connected to the right parties for achieving these kinds of gains, begin by identifying your most useful contacts. The following list will give you some idea of where to start.

- Labor union leaders.

- Legislative committees.

- Professional organizations.

- Lobbyists.

- Nonprofit political or environmental groups.

For more ideas, see Philip Howard's book *The Death of Common Sense: How Law Is Suffocating America.*

Sometimes organizations are forced to pay the price for crimes committed by others. Because there have been unscrupulous contractors, all builders must now submit to the slow and sometimes costly process of building inspections. Our government bureaucracies have developed largely in response to a few powerful, corrupt politicians. Recent advances in employee involvement efforts are running up against the 60-year-old National Labor Relations Act that was written to protect workers from employers' attempts to establish sham unions. In some cases these regulations have been kept on the books simply because no one has invested the time or energy to question them.

Here are some suggestions for examining the relevancy of your regulations and for taking action on those that can no longer truly be justified.

The regulation was created to resolve past abuses

- Work cooperatively with others in your industry.
- Demonstrate your ability to self-police.
- Work to abolish the regulation.

Work Cooperatively with Others in Your Industry

The purpose of most regulations is to assure that the rights of all are protected and to apply laws consistently to all stakeholders. Therefore your organization (unless it is a very large player in the game) probably will not have sufficient leverage or power to affect regulatory change by itself. Even if you could demonstrate that the regulation is unnecessary in your case, you probably would not be granted special dispensation. An important strategy, therefore, will be to join forces with others in your industry.

Begin by identifying the other key players and engaging them in dialogues about the regulations. Since this may involve partnering with competitors, you may need to establish some ground rules for working together that will protect each player's interests as well as ensure that you are not treading into any dangerous legal waters (antitrust issues, monopolies, price fixing). Ask all the stakeholders to identify and preferably quantify the impact (both positive and negative) of the regulations on their businesses and then brainstorm ways to meet the intent of the law in ways that minimize the cost or inconvenience to you.

Demonstrate Your Ability to Self-Police

Together, with the other key players, come to a common understanding of the intent of the regulation. Verify this understanding with the entity that has issued the regulation. Demonstrate that your organizations' values and goals are aligned with that intent and that your collective actions have been consistently within the letter of the regulation. (Note: If you or any of the other players cannot demonstrate this compliance, the regulation is probably not outdated. If you have been consistently in compliance while others have not, see "The Regulation is Being Used as an Excuse" earlier in this chapter.)

You and your colleagues should build a case for policing yourselves on the issue. Design outcomes that meet the intent of the regulation and the needs of the people whose interests it was designed to meet. Focusing on the intent—as opposed to the solution specified in the regulation—will leave you greater latitude for creative strategies. Include in your case a plan for how you will achieve those outcomes. It may be necessary to gradually shift the policing function from the regulatory agency to your own consortium. You will need to demonstrate your ability to fulfill your pledge in order to build the necessary trust with the community.

Work to Abolish the Regulation

Some well-intentioned regulations have become anachronisms in our times. Many states that implemented bottle bills in the 1970s to prevent litter now have curbside recycling programs. In some places consumers must haul to the store that which their garbage haulers can collect weekly at their curbs.

If self-policing is not a viable option, or if the regulation is clearly outdated and unnecessary, then the best course of action is to work to abolish the regulation. The cooperation of others in your industry as well as of key community and political leaders will be useful in this strategy. As part of building your case and your support for the change, you will need to demonstrate that the interests the regulations were meant to protect will not be violated. Your case should include a review of the data used to create the regulation in the first place as well as the more recent data that supports your stance. Since the cost of such a campaign could be high, be sure to calculate the potential return on your investment.

For more information, see Philip Howard's book *The Death of Common Sense: How Law Is Suffocating America.*

4. The Regulations Contradict Each Other

Some businesses and services impact so many sectors of our society that they are regulated by several different agencies, each with its own special area of concern. Though we'd like to think it never happens, there are occasions when the requirements of one agency contradict the requirements of another. During the construction of a biomedical research facility, for example, health officials required the contractors to install high-velocity exhaust systems that ran continuously to assure that the people who worked in the building could not be exposed to the germs and toxic agents with which they worked. The fire marshal, however, insisted that all mechanical systems be designed to automatically shut off in the event of a fire to prevent the spread of flames and gases. It's like one doctor prescribing dairy products for your ulcer and another ordering you to avoid them to lower your cholesterol. The contradictions can be maddening.

The regulations contradict each other

- Know the laws.
- Work collaboratively with regulating agencies.
- Work with others to develop consistent standards.

Know the Laws

The worst possible outcome is encountering contradictions, such as the one just described, after the fact. The best defense is to be educated about all the regulations that impact your business. In many cases this commitment may require expertise that you do not have. You will need to work with consultants or technical experts to assure that you have all the information you need to comply.

Work Collaboratively with Regulating Agencies

To help avoid contradictions and violations, many industries create cross-agency, problem-solving, or design teams that consist of representatives from the various regulating agencies. In the building industry, for example, architects frequently convene design teams that consist of designers, engineers, building officials, health department representatives, fire marshals, environmentalists, or geologists. It is easier to identify the various concerns and iron out the contradictions when all the key players are in the room together. This strategy relieves you from the burden of having to act as the messenger or go-between.

Work with Others to Develop Consistent Standards

It would be nice to think that all one has to do to resolve this problem is to bring contradictions or inconsistencies to the attention of the appropriate agencies. Since they are probably from separate arms of government, however, it is unlikely that the agencies have the infrastructure to coordinate and align their actions. You must decide how much effort to spend to take on the system. As suggested earlier, you can share the expense and effort by banding together with others in your industry to collect the evidence and present your case.

One of the down sides to rules and regulations is that they frequently inhibit healthy competition and other incentives to improve. This effect is especially obvious in regulated monopolies like utility companies or government services. In other cases regulations and controls are used as an excuse for less than exemplary performance. The solution is to shake up the system a little and get people thinking differently about how to operate within their legal obligations.

The regulations provide no incentive to improve

- Introduce competition.
- Tie future funding to outcomes.
- Give more control over the use of funds to those who do the work.

Introduce Competition

We are all familiar with the negative impact protectionist regulations have had on utilities. Think of the changes in service level and costs that have occurred since the telecommunication industry became a competitive business. Oddly enough, many organizations practice the same kind of protectionism within their own businesses. One hospital, for example, expected its physicians to use its in-house lab for all their tests. This practice was called into question when doctors discovered that they could get better, faster, and cheaper service from an outside source. The formerly complacent department of the hospital must now scramble to perform as well as the competition or face extinction. Government, too, is responding to the threat of competition. Many government services including garbage collection, road construction, and even corrections are now expected to meet or beat similar private-sector services.

Where the challenge of competition isn't realistic, at least encourage all functions or business units to benchmark against other like businesses. Sometimes this may mean looking outside your industry for best practices. In addition to benchmarking, all business functions should be surveying their customers (internal or external) on their level of satisfaction and their desire for improved or additional services.

Tie Future Funding to Outcomes

Another strategy for assuring improvement even where competition is absent is to tie financial support to measurable outcomes. The state of Oregon, for example, established a set of 272 measurable indicators of its strategic vision. Beginning in 1993 all state agencies were directed to develop performance measures tied to the benchmarks. Because the legislature uses the benchmarks to establish budget priorities, only those agencies that can show positive impact on the benchmarks are assured of funding.

The key to this practice is in the careful crafting of outcome measures. Oregon had to convince the federal government to redefine funding standards that were prescriptive and activity focused (number of services provided or the number of clients served) and to allow the state the latitude to determine its own process as long as it assured the achievement of outcomes. Today, for example, the Job Training Partnership Act is funded on the basis of the number of people who get jobs instead of the number of people who get job training.

Give More Control over the Use of Funds to Those Who Do the Work

 It's unrealistic to expect people or business units to be concerned with costs or quality if they have no control over either. Nearly everyone has had experience with the "spend it or lose it" rule for departmental budgets. This mentality represents a flagrant disincentive to save money. Many organizations, both public and private, are experimenting with eliminating restrictions on budget allocations. Save it and invest it is the new paradigm. Mission-driven budgeting, as it is called, empowers departments or agencies to pursue their missions by liberating them from constraining budget categories. Instead departments are encouraged to create budgets for the purpose of tracking and analyzing how money is used, but they have the freedom to spend money where it is needed to cover unexpected expenses and to take advantage of unanticipated opportunities. They keep every dollar that they save.

This system not only encourages efficiency and ownership but also is simpler to manage, frees up resources to test new ideas, makes a department more flexible and responsive, and frees the strategic decision makers to focus on the big issues instead of managing the minutiae.

For examples of this process, see Osborne and Gaebler's *Reinventing Government.*

17 Involuntary Alliances

Critical stakeholders will not allow us to do what we need to be successful.

You never got to choose the genes you were born with, and these will have a major impact on your longevity. Similarly in organizations, we are all subject to alliances we did not have the power to choose. An organization may be owned by a parent company in a different country. Managers do not select the unions that represent their employees. Government agencies and educational institutions are greatly affected by the people we vote into office. A utility company cannot choose whether a public utility commission has control over its pricing. If you're trapped in the gorilla cage, make friends with the gorilla.

Review the following symptoms to determine a likely cause of your problem. Then turn to the pages describing the cause to identify a course of action.

Symptoms

Each stakeholder seems to want something different and diametrically opposed from the others. (1, 4)

Stakeholders don't seem willing to take the time to resolve the situation. (3)

Stakeholders' requirements seem unreasonable. (2, 4)

Stakeholders can't seem to agree on much of anything. (4, 5)

Stakeholders are "bad-mouthing" one another. (5, 6)

Stakeholders seem unwilling to change. (6)

Stakeholders aren't talking to one another. (5, 6)

Causes

1. Conflicting needs of stakeholders.

2. Key stakeholders don't understand our needs.

3. You're low on the stakeholders' priority lists.

4. Strong value differences.

5. History of mistrust.

6. Playing politics.

R_X

When the needs of stakeholders appear to be diametrically opposed, cooperation is unlikely. Unfortunately, as long as this stalemate continues, the parties' ability to solve the problem lessens. People tend to become more entrenched in their positions, less willing to hear other views, and less able to craft a collaborative solution that meets everyone's needs.

In these situations, bringing the parties together in a neutral place can help them deal with the dissonance, but care must be taken not to force a premature decision. For example, a town in Washington was facing the shutdown of its primary employer—a smelter—owing to environmental hazards. People in the town sported buttons labeled "Jobs" or "Health" depending upon their persuasion. The head of the EPA resisted the temptation to force a decision, something he had the power to do. Instead, he led the community in a dialogue. After a while, the community realized that linking its future to any one industry was imprudent and shifted its focus to economic diversity. Then the buttons read "Both." [1]

Finding a higher ground among conflicting stakeholder interests takes time and patience. A few of the methods in this chapter help to identify common ground or a shared purpose. The other methods provide a way to identify positive steps that at least do not nullify the actions of the other stakeholders, even if the stakeholders do not view themselves as seeking the same end.

Conflicting needs of stakeholders ➤

- Conduct a future-search conference.
- Seek to resolve the apparent paradox.
- Identify a higher common purpose.
- Establish a decision-making council of key stakeholders.

---

1 H. Lee, "Managing Environmental Risk: The Case of Asarco," John F. Kennedy School of Government Case Program, Harvard University, 1985.

Conduct a Future-Search Conference

Marvin Weisbord's future-search-conference methods are effective for finding common ground among diverse stakeholders. While no two search conferences are the same, the generic model involves bringing all stakeholders (or representatives of all stakeholders) together for a two (or more) day conference. The participants explore the past, examine the challenges of the present, and develop a preferred future (hence the name "future search"). For more information, see *Future Search*, *Productive Workplaces*, and *Discovering Common Ground* by Marvin Weisbord.

Seek to Resolve the Apparent Paradox

The government sector often has the most difficulty resolving conflicting needs because its customers are often one of its involuntary alliances. For example, how does a transportation department build a road so the drivers can enjoy the view of the river and simultaneously shield the rafters/kayakers from a view of the cars? Both are legitimate needs, and unlike business, the agency cannot choose to serve only one set of customers.

Conflicts are especially common where the person who uses a service is not the one who pays (e.g., health care, AFDC, HUD). Bridging the gap between these two groups goes a long way toward resolving the problems. Giving the users choice in providers, vouchers for services, or requiring co-payments are all examples of strategies that have worked in certain situations. See *Reinventing Government* by Osborne and Gaebler for more information.

Regardless of the source of the conflict, you can sometimes resolve the paradox. Often needs appear to be in conflict only because we cannot envision a way to satisfy them all simultaneously. We used to think in terms of quality versus cost or environmental responsibility versus profits. Now we can envision these as compatible goals.

A variety of discussion methods can help people "think outside the box." Dialogue (Peter Senge), the six thinking hats (Edward de Bono), and breakthrough thinking methods (Nadler and Hibino) all provide useful models. The trick is to get people thinking in terms of *and*, not *or*: What would it look like if we could satisfy X *and* Y?

Identify a Higher Common Purpose

People often argue about specifics even when they agree on the overarching purpose or goal. Many people argue about whether abortion should be legal or what to include in sex education. Practically everyone agrees, however, that reducing unwanted pregnancies is a good goal. Instead of recognizing our common ground, we waste enormous energy fighting over strategy.

Creating a purpose hierarchy can help adversaries identify their common purpose. Ask each party to state its position and list it on the bottom of a flip chart. Then repeatedly ask why it takes that view and list the answers higher and higher on the page. Then compare the lists from the various stakeholders. They may range from quite prescriptive (put condom vending machines in schools) to lofty (make the world a better place).

You can usually find common ground somewhere in the lists. Then all stakeholders must grant the others the freedom to pursue their common purpose in their own way. If trust is not adequate for this freedom to be granted, suggest a period of experimentation with a review date sometime in the future. Develop methods for tracking and measuring progress. After the experimentation period, come back together to review what you have learned about your impacts on one another. For more information on purpose hierarchies, see *Breakthrough Thinking* by Nadler and Hibino. See also "Use Systems Thinking to Identify How You Are Affecting Each Other" later in this chapter.

Establish a Decision-Making Council of Key Stakeholders

 If stakeholder needs are clearly opposed, establish a mechanism for negotiating the trade-offs between them. If this balancing of interests must occur on an on-going basis, a cross-functional council can be given decision-making authority to resolve disagreements. For example, several cities formed

such councils to guide them out of financial difficulties. In these councils, interest-based negotiating skills are paramount. See *Getting to Yes: Negotiating Agreement without Giving In* by Fisher and Ury as well as *Getting Past No: Negotiating with Difficult People* by William Ury. See also *Breakthrough Thinking* by Nadler and Hibino for helpful group decision-making tools.

Stakeholders are often too far removed to understand your needs. Union officials may not understand the impact their decisions have on the bottom line. A parent company may not comprehend how their new compensation system will hurt your operation. Legislators may not be close enough to the operation to forecast how a new law may affect you. You must be proactive.

Key stakeholders don't understand our needs

- Educate the stakeholders on the situation.
- Bring stakeholders closer to the work.
- Use technology to help keep distant stakeholders informed and involved.

Educate the Stakeholders on the Situation

One option is to educate the stakeholders on your situation. Presentations and educational sessions may be helpful. Use your stockholder meetings, annual reports, and other communication opportunities to inform stakeholders of your challenges. One high-tech firm that won its state quality award meets quarterly with the mayor and city council to brief local officials on its business plan and progress.

Use lobbyists to carry your message to influential members of the government. You can also involve them in your planning and goal setting by using conference models such as future-search conferences (Weisbord) and real-time strategic change (Jacobs). See the section on involving partners in goal setting and planning in the next chapter for more information.

Educating stakeholders is the foundation of community-policing programs, where stronger alliances are built between the community and its law enforcement agencies. In this setting, police spend a significant amount of time attending neighborhood-association meetings, leading neighborhood-watch groups, making presentations in schools, and participating in recreational events with youth.

Bring Stakeholders Closer to the Work

Nothing compares with hands-on knowledge. Where possible, bring the stakeholders closer to the work. Invite them to visit your site; have them talk to employees and customers; show them the impacts of their decisions. Where possible, get them involved in the real work such as requiring board members to volunteer their time on the job or using teachers as interns in industry. Some organizations, such as Northrop and Baxter Healthcare, have offered free training to their key community stakeholders. At a minimum, you can invite stakeholders for site visits to learn about your process and problems first hand.

In global corporations, rotating managers through various key countries gives them an intimate understanding of the diverse cultures and practices within the organization. Assignments should last at least one year to overcome cultural biases and language barriers.

Use Technology to Help Keep Distant Stakeholders Informed and Involved

Distance must be bridged. The farther away stakeholders are from your operation, the more difficulty they will have understanding your needs. Use all the technological tools at your disposal such as teleconferencing, Internet, e-mail, and faxes. Investigate the use of "groupware" interactive software that facilitates meetings and project work among geographically separated team members.

3. You're Low on the Stakeholders' Priority Lists

The CEO of a *Fortune* 100 company isn't going to spend a lot of time focusing on a tiny subsidiary buried within the family of companies. In today's busy world, everyone practices a form of triage, focusing on the items with the biggest payback and ignoring the rest. If you're a small fish in your stakeholders' ponds, you'll have to work harder to get their attention.

You're low on the stakeholders' priority lists

- Link your actions to stakeholders' primary strategies.
- Ask for more free rein to experiment.
- Break the alliance.

Link Your Actions to Stakeholders' Primary Strategies

Showing how your needs and goals align with those of key stakeholders may help to elevate you in priority. First seek to understand the perspective of your stakeholders. Clarify the hidden needs that lie below their stated positions. Probe for the gap between what they want and what they have. Then build a sense of urgency by exploring the costs of their inaction; what are the costs of doing nothing? Finally, show how meeting your needs helps to satisfy theirs as well. See *SPIN Selling* and *Major Account Sales Strategy* by Neil Rackham for excellent tools and concepts.

Ask for More Free Rein to Experiment

If you can't appear any bigger in the pond, the opposite strategy often works. De-emphasize your importance and ask for more freedom. After all, the risks are small. Just as a money manager might speculate with a small percentage of an investment portfolio, your stakeholders might be willing to take more risks with a small fish. Be prepared to make a strong business case for your independence and be sure to demonstrate your ability to operate responsibly with less supervision.

Break the Alliance

If the above strategies don't work and you are not able to get adequate support, one option to consider is to break the alliance (more easily done with some stakeholders than others, of course). Obviously, the specific action will depend on who the stakeholders are. Some governmental agencies are privatizing to release themselves of stifling civil-service procedures. A floundering division might become a star on its own or as part of another organization. A regulated industry can be deregulated. Unions are occasionally decertified.

One word of caution: As with any divorce, make sure you are not just taking your problems with you. Unforeseen consequences always accompany any radical change. If you choose this option of last resort, make sure you have thought through all the issues.

4. Strong Value Differences

Values and beliefs are at the root of most long-standing disagreements, and both are extremely difficult to change. Consequently, the best strategy is often to promote understanding and acceptance. When others feel you are not trying to change their values, they may grant you the same freedom.

Strong value differences

- Share cultural differences and promote the value of diversity.

- Use job rotation across organizational boundaries to develop understanding.

- Use systems thinking to identify how you are affecting each other.

- Develop a needs matrix that focuses on solutions that meet all or the majority of stakeholder needs.

Share Cultural Differences and Promote the Value of Diversity

Just as the fish does not contemplate the water in which it swims, people do not often think about their values and beliefs. They just act on them and assume that others share the same sets of beliefs. In our increasingly diverse workplace and global marketplace, this assumption is dangerous.

Talking openly about cultural differences goes a long way toward developing understanding and acceptance. Diversity training is a good place to begin. The Center for Creative Leadership has developed a seven-dimension model of cultural diversity (only one type of diversity). Discussing the following attributes may be revealing:

• Sources of identity (individual versus collective)

• Methods of achievement (assertive versus supportive)

• Response to authority (equal versus unequal)

• Orientation to opportunity (dynamic versus stable)

• Means of knowledge acquisition (active versus reflective)

• Perspectives on time (scarce versus plentiful)

• Outlook on life (doing versus being)[2]

---

2. M. Wilson, "The Intercultural Values Questionnaire," *Issues and Observations* 15, no. 1, p. 10.

We also recommend discussing such questions as:

• What are your attitudes toward authority and power?

• What role does conflict play in the workplace?

• How do you prefer to deal with conflict?

• What are your attitudes toward working in teams versus working individually?

• What do you believe is true about most people in the workplace? What motivates them? What do they need from their leaders? What do they get out of work?

• What is the best workplace you've experienced, and what was so special about it?

See "Different from What? Diversity as a Performance Issue" by Jack Gordon, and *The Managing Diversity Survival Kit* by Gardenswartz and Rowe for tools and tips.

Use Job Rotation across Organizational Boundaries to Develop Understanding

Nothing compares with hands-on knowledge. Where possible, bring the stakeholders inside to do the work. This might involve long-term transfers or temporary assignments to relieve bottlenecks. For example, architectural firms frequently will share employees with each other to balance work loads. Think of your organization as having permeable walls.

Use Systems Thinking to Identify How You Are Affecting Each Other

In cases where you cannot identify common ground with stakeholders, you may still be able to call a truce on mutually destructive behavior. Even wars have rules that benefit both sides.

First, you must analyze the cycle of actions. Airline A drops its rates and Airlines B, C, and D follow suit. Then Airline A must drop its rates again. Drawing this as a perpetuating cycle helps people to understand how their actions hurt themselves as well as their "adversaries." Seek to understand not the simple cause and effect but rather the larger system at work. Where you are not able to discuss these cycles openly (where it would be considered collusion), you can at least seek to act in ways that improve the playing field for all. See the following articles on game theory and its application in business: "Games Businesses Play" by Rita Koselka and "Winning the Game of Business" by Rob Norton.

You can also use system thinking to build collaborative relationships. For example, if your union is focused on job security and management is focused on profits, you can draw cycles of actions that lead toward both.

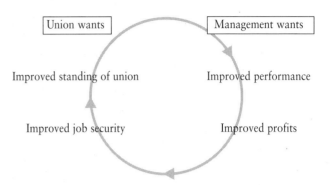

Proposal: Develop high-performance teams

Union wants — Management wants

Improved standing of union — Improved performance

Improved job security — Improved profits

Conversely, you can diagram how one party's actions have been hurting the other and then coming back to hurt themselves. See chapters 4 and 5 in *The Fifth Discipline* by Peter Senge for a discussion of systems diagrams.

Develop a Needs Matrix that Focuses on Solutions that Meet All or the Majority of Stakeholder Needs

One technique that helps to identify the optimal path between conflicting needs is to build a needs matrix. List all stakeholders across the top of a matrix. Then have each stakeholder group brainstorm solutions and select a few options that are worthy of consideration; list those down the left side of the matrix. Then compare each idea to each stakeholder group, using a plus (+), minus (-), or zero (0) to indicate whether each stakeholder would view the idea as positive, negative, or neutral. When the chart is complete, select the options that have the fewest minus signs.

Option/Stakeholders	Management	Union	Employees	Stockholders
Layoff employees	–	–	–	+
Reduce wages across the board	0	–	–	–
Reduce hours (mandatory cutbacks)	–	–	+	0
Reduce hours (voluntary cutbacks)	–	0	+	0

A variation on this idea is to use information from a purpose hierarchy. Each stakeholder group develops a purpose hierarchy (described earlier in this chapter), working upward from its position by asking why and downward by asking how. From the top part of its hierarchy (the *why*'s), each group should identify its must-haves; list those along the top of the matrix. Then each group picks actions from the bottom half of its hierarchy (the *how*'s); list those down the left side. Then do the analysis as explained in the previous section. See *Breakthrough Thinking* by Nadler and Hibino for more information on the purpose hierarchy. See also *The Catalytic Leadership Handbook* by Hitchcock, Willard, and Warnock.

A few pointers for using this technique: Establish the ground rule that everyone has the right to ask for what they need but that you shouldn't ask for more than you need. Be sure that the selected options are adequate to meet the needs of the situation.

5. History of Mistrust

Unfortunately, mistrust is rampant within organizations for various reasons. Organizational resources are wasted as people cover their backsides, incite coups, and gossip about old wounds. We highlight a few strategies for overcoming mistrust, but please see the following resources for more assistance: *Driving Fear out of the Workplace* by Ryan and Oestreich and *Healing the Wounds* by David Noer.

Past history of mistrust

- Admit past mistakes.
- Share information openly.
- Use a mediator to resolve past conflicts.
- Develop a contract for future action and follow through.

Admit Past Mistakes

Face up to past transgressions and apologize. Even if the transgressions were more perceived than real, this is a good strategy.

Share Information Openly

Far too much information is considered confidential in organizations. This attitude only breeds mistrust. Open the books, open office doors, openly discuss organizational challenges. Some organizations even make salaries public information. Challenge your assumptions about what employees "should not know." Some organizations may find it hard to share information openly because of assumptions about employees' trustworthiness or maturity. See *Maverick* by Ricardo Semler for a description of an extremely open organization.

Use a Mediator to Resolve Past Conflicts

If the past is fraught with bad, painful experiences, a trained mediator can help individuals or groups work through them to build more positive future relationships. One good model for healing is Blake and Mouton's "interface conflict-solving model" described in *Solving Costly Organizational Conflicts*. After identifying who is on which side, follow these steps that alternate between the sides doing tasks alone and working together:

1. Each side describes the optimal relationship.
2. The sides share and consolidate their ideas.
3. Each side describes the actual, current relationship.
4. The sides share and consolidate.
5. Jointly, the sides plan and contract for change.
6. After a period of time, the sides hold a progress review.

Focusing on the optimal relationship first is an important psychological component to this process. To find a trained mediator, we suggest asking the following sources: your state's mediators board, the Better Business Bureau, your employee assistance program, and your local attorney referral service. Since mediators tend to specialize, find one with experience in the specific area of dispute.

Develop a Contract for Future Action and Follow Through

You build trust when you say what you mean and do what you say, so be explicit about what you will do and then follow through. Write down your agreements and plan formal evaluation sessions to review how the relationship is going. Also, develop ground rules about how you will work together. One ground rule ought to be taken from the Hippocratic oath: Do no harm.

6. Playing Politics

When people place their personal interests (or those of their constituents) over the interests of the greater good, we say they are "playing politics." Not only does this behavior lead to ill will, bickering, and wasted energy fighting one another; it reduces the parties' ability to resolve future problems. This reduced future capacity is in no one's best interest.

Playing politics

- Seek win–win solutions.
- Conduct a stakeholder analysis to identify who wil! work for or against you.
- Engage early adopters and innovators who will be inclined to support change.

Seek Win–Win Solutions

The first option should always be to seek win–win solutions, not mediocre compromises. To do this, you must reveal the interests behind the stated positions, and you must treat the other party with respect. See the various books published about the Harvard Negotiation Project including *Getting Past No* by William Ury and *Getting to Yes* by Fisher and Ury. Also see the following articles on game theory and its application in business: "Games Businesses Play" by Rita Koselka and "Winning the Game of Business" by Rob Norton.

Conduct a Stakeholder Analysis to Identify Who Will Work for or against You

In planning your strategy, it is often helpful to conduct a stakeholder analysis that examines who is likely to be supportive or unsupportive, and helps you develop strategies for getting them on board. You can use a chart similar to the one that follows to identify where key stakeholders are now (on a scale from "make it happen" to "stop it") and then draw arrows to represent where you need to move them. Usually your focus will be on moving people to the left but sometimes you need to get someone to be less invested in the outcome.

Stakeholder	Make It Happen	Help It Happen	Let It Happen	Resist It	Stop It	Suggested Action
Jane Doe		←	←	•		Involve her in the planning.
Dale Vu	•	→				Encourage him to let the champion take the lead; keep a lower profile.
Union			←	←	•	Make them partners in the process; guarantee no layoffs for two years.

Engage Early Adopters and Innovators Who Will Be Inclined to Support Change

People often need proof that an idea will work before they are willing to support it. Within any population, some people will be "early adopters," eager to try something new. One strategy is to seek out one or more of these early adopters and ask them to pilot the idea quietly and unobtrusively. Then when significant benefits have been documented, ask for public support. To make this plan work, you will need credible performance measures. See Chapter 8 on measures if needed.

18 Voluntary Alliances

Our "partners" are inhibiting our progress.

Just as you have control over many things that affect your health (such as diet, exercise, not smoking), you also choose many relationships that may affect your organization's well-being. Not all alliances are involuntary. You can, in most cases, choose your suppliers. Businesses can pick their customers and markets. You can choose the source of financing. You may even establish joint ventures and other strategic alliances that help you leverage synergies.

Whenever you are working with another entity, you have the possibility of conflicts of interest and misunderstandings. Here are the most common causes of headaches that these alliances face.

Symptoms

Your partners aren't giving you what you need when you need it. (1, 2)

Your partners cannot seem to meet your expectations consistently. (1, 2)

Your partners seem hesitant to do what you need. (1, 3)

Causes

1. Partners don't understand your needs.

2. Partners are struggling to meet your needs.

3. Partners can't meet your needs without hurting themselves.

Many of the actions for involuntary alliances may also apply, so if you don't find what you need in this list, review the previous chapter.

Strategic alliances are becoming increasingly popular as organizations become more networked. We suggest these three resources for anyone considering or forming such an alliance:

• *Partnerships for Profit: Structuring and Managing Strategic Alliances* by Jordan Lewis.

• "Putting More Strategy into Strategic Alliances" by Rigby and Buchanan.

• "A Four-Step Process for Creating Alliances" by Abram Bluestein.

1. Partners Don't Understand Your Needs

Many problems in alliances stem from simple misunderstandings and assumptions. Building shared understanding within an organization is hard enough; doing it across organizational boundaries takes even more effort. Here are some strategies which work effectively.

Partners don't understand your needs

- Explore needs and expectations.
- Offer site visits.
- Lease employees to partners.
- Offer joint training sessions.
- Involve partners in goal setting and planning.
- Make partners formal members of the team.

Explore Needs and Expectations

Clarify and negotiate expectations. Using surveys, focus groups, and open discussions, seek to understand the other stakeholders' priorities. One simple process is to assemble your stakeholders or stakeholder groups and ask them these questions:

- Where are we not meeting your expectations? How would our performance need to change to meet your expectations?

- Where are we meeting your expectations? Do you expect your needs to increase, decrease, or stay the same in the near future?

- Where are we exceeding your expectations? Is it important to you that we continue to do so?

Where the trade-offs are complex, the "house of quality" process can be helpful (see "The House of Quality" by Hauser and Clausing). This process can be used to clarify the trade-offs between interdependent variables such as gas efficiency, crash tests, and solid "feel" of a car door.

Offer Site Visits

Nothing compares to being there. So make a regular practice of visiting each other's sites, talking to people at all levels, and observing the work. People at all levels of the organization—executives, frontline employees, and everyone else in between—should make these visits. Arrange for both structured and unstructured time. We suggest the following structure for a three-hour site visit:

- **Host presentation.** What do you do? How does your partner's product or service affect you? Whom do you serve? What is difficult about what you do? What are your plans for the future?

- **Site tour.** Break into small groups (of six to eight people) with a host leader. Plan the routes so you won't all converge at the same place at the same time. Give the tour leaders a list of key points to cover on the walk-through. Guests should be careful not to disrupt the work or write notes while touring.

- **Panel/questions and answers.** Have an open discussion of observations, issues, questions, etc.

Lease Employees to Partners

Even better than site visits is leasing your employees to your partners. The employees can actually do the work and become intimately knowledgeable about your partners issues. If you schedule this process during your slow periods and your stakeholder's peak times, this cooperative use of human resources can also help to reduce bottlenecks and handle workload variations across organizations. For example, architectural firms routinely share architects to cover their peaks and valleys.

Offer Joint Training Sessions

Partners need a common language, and it's helpful if they use similar processes. One way to achieve this is to offer joint training sessions that representatives from all the partner organizations can attend. In addition to spreading training costs, joint training builds shared understanding. You can also fill extra seats in your training sessions with members of your partner organizations. See "Training Consortia: How They Work and How They Don't" by Bob Filipczak.

Involve Partners in Goal Setting and Planning

Until recently, suppliers were often treated as adversaries. Organizations tried to get the best deal, so they withheld information and went out for competitive bids. This approach has hidden costs, which practices such as just-in-time manufacturing have revealed. Many organizations are now treating their suppliers and customers as partners, involving them in goal setting. See *Real-Time Strategic Change* by Robert Jacobs for one such method. Sometimes partners are even given access to sensitive data that links them directly into the organization's information systems. For example, retailers may be directly linked to their suppliers in order to maintain appropriate inventory levels.

Make Partners Formal Members of the Team

Some organizations have been able to make customers and suppliers formal members of their team, having a full-time member from the partner firm on site. Since geographic distance is a key determinant of the frequency of communication, this powerful strategy results in creative synergies. In our increasingly "boundaryless" organizations, this practice is becoming more common. Of course, if you cannot justify having a full-time member on site, you may still be able to bring the partners in for team meetings or other special events.

2. Partners Are Struggling to Meet Your Needs

That partners understand your needs does not automatically lead to their being able to meet your needs. It is in your best interest to help them. The key to dealing with partners is effective "partnering."

For example, ADC Kentrox, a manufacturer of telecommunications equipment and winner of the 1994 Oregon Quality Award, partners heavily with its vendors. Suppliers are involved in product design reviews to discuss requirements and improvements. Kentrox tracks and shares vendor performance information such as pricing, delivery, quality, and service. Some of its suppliers work on site. Kentrox's formal supplier-development process includes
- Initial surveys.
- Sharing monthly lot acceptance data.
- Free training.
- Supplier-of-the-year award.

Partners are struggling to meet your needs

- Offer joint training sessions.
- Require that your partners implement quality systems to ensure consistency.
- Build in a feedback loop for corrective action.

Offer Joint Training Sessions

Often suppliers, especially small businesses, do not have as many resources available to them as you may have. Inviting them to training and educational events is one way to help them. Partners need a common language, and it's helpful if they use similar processes. One way to achieve this shared language is to offer joint training sessions that representatives from all the partner organizations can attend. In addition to spreading training costs, joint training builds shared understanding. You can also fill extra seats in your training sessions with members of your partner organizations. See "Training Consortia: How They Work and How They Don't" by Bob Filipczak.

Require That Your Partners Implement Quality Systems to Ensure Consistency

You have a right to expect consistent quality from all your partners, and you should ask them to explain how that is being ensured. ISO certification is one appropriate response. In our opinion, however, you should not be prescriptive about the methods your partners use to achieve consistency (such as requiring all your suppliers to submit applications for the Malcolm Baldrige Award or demanding ISO certification). Being prescriptive often leads to the supplier complying with the requirement (submitting the application) without meeting the ultimate intent (providing consistent quality).

Build in a Feedback Loop for Corrective Action

Examine the processes that connect your partners with your organization and identify common or critical problems that can occur. Then make sure you have a timely, fail-safe feedback loop to address any problems. Some organizations return problem cards to suppliers. In some cases, an immediate phone call is in order.

In our opinion, both Bell Atlantic and American Express have excellent supplier assessment and feedback mechanisms. The assessment is based on the criteria from the Baldrige Award, and it provides suppliers with a detailed evaluation of their business processes and results. Both companies offer gold, silver, and bronze awards to their top suppliers based on the assessment.

Your body depends on a symbiotic relationship with other organisms that live in you and on you, just as your organization depends on a symbiotic relationship with your partners. But partners can't be parasites. If, by meeting your needs, your partners are growing weaker, eventually you both will suffer. In today's turbulent world, however, the burden may not be equally shared between the partners. First, you should seek ways to mitigate the inequities. The final option, of course, is to dissolve the partnership.

Partners can't meet your needs without hurting themselves

- Develop strategic alliances that benefit both partners.
- Dissolve the partnership.

Develop Strategic Alliances That Benefit Both Partners

Just-in-time manufacturing is one method that tends to transfer a burden from customer to supplier. The supplier may need to make multiple deliveries during a week when a monthly shipment may have been the norm. This requirement has the potential of increasing the supplier's costs. To make matters worse, the customer may also insist on price concessions on top of the increased service.

The only way to make this and other strategic alliances viable over the long term is to work cooperatively to find ways to benefit the supplier as well. Making it a sole-source provider, giving it access to your inventory database, and reducing the administrative costs associated with servicing the account are all valid areas to consider. See *Partnerships for Profit: Structuring and Managing Strategic Alliances* by Jordan Lewis, "Putting More Strategy into Strategic Alliances" by Rigby and Buchanan, and "A Four-Step Process for Creating Alliances" by Abram Bluestein. See also "Seek to Resolve the Apparent Paradox" and "Seek Win–Win Solutions" in Chapter 17.

Dissolve the Partnership

The option of last resort is to dissolve the partnership. This usually involves seeking other suppliers or customers. We are not recommending breaking the terms of a contract but rather waiting until the term elapses. To do otherwise is to elicit an ugly divorce with all the associated costs. However, even under the best of circumstances, breaking off a long-term relationship is hard, and you will need to invest significant time in building a new one.

Instead of seeking other suppliers, one option is to diversify vertically, pulling into the organization the tasks that used to be done by partners. However, given the pace of change, this option is increasingly unattractive.

19 Global Trends

The future does not bode well for us.

We know more about promoting good health than we ever have before. What we are learning, however, is not always welcome information. It was a lot more fun to eat ice cream before we knew that it clogs our arteries. Ignoring this information, as tempting as it may be, can be disastrous. So it is with organizations who fail to heed the trends that impact their businesses. Though it may not always be pleasant, the first step is to acknowledge and accept the trends. People can easily brush aside data that doesn't fit their mental models of how the world is operating. Think of the mistakes made by the Big Three automakers, IBM, the Swiss watchmakers, and even those made at Pearl Harbor. The focus of this chapter is on helping organizations discover and understand the relevant trends. Once you have done that, you may need to reevaluate your strategy, which cycles you back to the beginning of this book.

Symptoms

We never seem prepared for changes in our external environment. (1, 2)

We're not sure what the future of our business is. (1, 2, 3)

Other organizations seem to respond to external events faster and more effectively than we do. (1, 2)

Causes

1. We don't know what the trends are.

2. People are ignoring the trends.

3. Current strategy is not appropriate for the future.

261

1. We Don't Know What the Trends Are

Like the ostrich that never knew what hit him, you've got to pull your head out of the sand and take a hard look at the horizon to avoid getting nailed. It takes effort and discipline, but it is usually more expensive and exasperating to be just one step ahead of a crisis. If your organization seems to be running as fast as it can just to keep up, consider the strategies suggested here to gain a better hold on your future.

We don't know what the trends are

- Conduct an environmental scan.
- Benchmark.

Conduct an Environmental Scan

While no one has a reliable crystal ball, plenty of clues are still available about what the future holds for you. The trick is to be dedicated and disciplined about studying them. Your research should be directed by a comprehensive set of questions:

- What are your customers expectations regarding your product or service and how are those likely to change in the future?

- What standards do your customers use to judge your products or services and how will those likely change?

- What technological advances will affect your business?

- What political, legal, social, and environmental developments will affect your business?

Consider some of the strategies in the following list to help you and your organization stay on top of the trends and issues that will affect your business.

- Attend international conferences. Certainly those conferences related to your industry will be critical, but also try to include conferences that focus on peripheral issues such as current management and business practices, economic and trade patterns, environmental issues, or education and workforce development trends.

- Implement a clipping process. Contract with a clipping service to scan research and literature on several chosen topics or implement a clipping process within your own organization. You can do this fairly efficiently by dividing your areas of concern and the appropriate resources

among a team that is accountable for locating and sharing pertinent information.

- Surf the Internet. The Internet is fast becoming the largest single source of data in the world. On-line services enable you to conduct focused literature searches, connect with others on various topics, and access experts in a variety of fields from all around the world.

Whatever strategy you choose to conduct your research, be sure that you have the infrastructure to support the dissemination and application of the information you gather. (See Chapter 15 for additional help.) For more information on conducting environmental scans, see William Pasmore's book *Designing Effective Organizations* or for resources on futurism, see Peter Block's *Liberation Management*.

Benchmark

Your research should also include gathering information on your competitors and other "best practices" organizations. This process, called benchmarking, asks the question: How well are we performing relative to other organizations? There are three types of benchmarking:

- Internal benchmarking examines processes or practices within your own organization. Variances in performance or outputs from similar parts of one organization (matching departments at different sites or identical processes on different lines) make clear opportunities for improvement.

Internal benchmarking is also a way to share learning and information across the organization. (See also Chapter 15 on shared learning.)

- Competitive benchmarking involves examining the processes or products of your competition. When targeting organizations to benchmark be sure to include both the market leaders as well as the new entrants to the field. Sometimes the newer companies have the most innovative technologies and ideas. Because your competitors may be reluctant to share ideas that may be giving them a competitive advantage, you may need to rely on industry statistics or third-party benchmarking services. You are, however, certainly free to talk to your competitors' customers. While not privy to the inner workings of your competitors, they certainly can tell you a lot about what they do and don't value about the products and services they are getting.

- World-class benchmarking involves comparing a function or process in your organization to a similar function or process in a world-class organization. Because many business processes apply across industries, your targeted company may also be in another business. This situation will make it easier to access information.

For more information on benchmarking, see one of the following resources: *Benchmarking: The Search for Industry Best Practices That Lead to Superior Performance* by Robert Camp, *Improving through Benchmarking: A Practical Guide* by Richard Chang, or *The Benchmarking Book* by Michael Spendolini.

2. People Are Ignoring the Trends

Even when information is readily available, people will often choose to ignore it—like the belligerent smoker with the chronic cough. For some it's a matter of "information anxiety"; too much to process and comprehend. Others simply prefer to keep their heads in the sand, especially if the information conflicts with their beliefs or wishes. While these attitudes may be understandable, they are simply not acceptable—especially when the survival of your organization is at stake. Review the following strategies to see if any might remedy this situation in your own company.

People are ignoring the trends

- Involve people in evaluating trends.
- Allow people time to grieve for the past.
- Develop and communicate a case for change.
- Do scenario planning.

Involve People in Evaluating Trends

People are less intimidated by information or knowledge that they have had a hand in generating. Involving people in your trend analysis is also a way to enhance understanding. Another advantage of involving employees is the increased number of response ideas that can be generated. The leaders of a food products plant, for example, examined their future and could only see doom. They were predicting a plant closure. The employees had a different view of the situation. Their response was to come up with a new product idea that not only kept the plant open but also slightly repositioned the company in the marketplace.

Future-search conferences are becoming a popular means for involving large numbers of employees in analyzing trends and shaping vision. For more information on how to conduct a future-search conference, see Marvin Weisbord's book *Future Search*.

Allow People Time to Grieve for the Past

An important part of the process of accepting new ideas and change is taking time to release and grieve for the old ways. Unless you acknowledge the losses that people are feeling, you will likely meet with resistance to new ways. These losses may stem from any one of the following sources: personal attachments or sentimental feelings about traditions or other people, a connection to self-esteem, a sense of powerlessness or loss of control, or a loss of direction or confusion about the future.

The best strategy in this process is to acknowledge the feelings as they arise. Focus conversation on the problems instead of on any one suggested solution. You will know that people are ready to move on and accept new ideas when they demonstrate one or more of the following behaviors:

- They stopped lamenting the past and continually referring to it.

- They stop grasping at simple, familiar solutions.

- They acknowledge the problem being faced.

For more information, see *Managing Transitions: Making the Most from Change* by William Bridges.

Develop and Communicate a Case for Change

Sometimes ideas or information will meet with resistance because the rationale or relevance is unclear. When sharing trend information be sure to communicate why it is important to the person receiving it. The intent is not just to shake up people with grim news but to get them excited about the future and where the organization could go. Consider the following tips for building a case for change:

- Identify the critical, strategic issues facing your organization (e.g., the need for efficiency or the need to improve quality or employee satisfaction).

- Determine your current ability to meet those issues.

- Identify the root causes of your (in)ability to meet your challenges.

- Calculate the effect and cost of not meeting your challenges.

- Create a shared vision of the desired future.

A new strategy for effectively implementing change is called real-time strategic planning. For more information, see *Real-Time Strategic Change* by Robert Jacobs.

Do Scenario Planning

 Another strategy for getting people to acknowledge and respond to trend data is to force them to grapple with it. Shell Oil discovered an effective method for conducting strategic forecasting, which it calls scenario planning. The process challenges participants to respond to a variety of scenarios or "what-if" situations. In creating their responses, participants must consider how they would manage under different paths to the future. The exercise effectively exposes and tests peoples' assumptions and generates creative ideas not possible in more traditional planning approaches. Technology and computer simulations that can quickly present and process thousands of variables and alternatives enhance this process. For more information on scenario planning, see *Competing for the Future* by Hamel and Prahalad. Also see the articles "Scenarios: Uncharted Waters Ahead" and "Scenarios: Shooting the Rapids" by Pierre Wack.

3. Our Current Strategy Is Not Appropriate for the Future

Sometimes the result of our efforts to understand the trends is a recognition that our current direction will completely miss the mark. We jog three miles every day to make our hearts strong only to learn that we are pulverizing our knees. If this is the case for your organization, you must first accept the fact that you are utilizing the wrong strategy and then reformulate your plan to meet the demands of your future.

Current strategy is not appropriate for the future

- **Reevaluate your strategy—Go back to Part I.**

Problem Analysis Worksheet

You'd probably consider yourself lucky if you only had one problem to deal with in your organization. More often, however, you may be struggling with multiple difficulties. Some of these may be interrelated. And perhaps, if you choose wisely, the actions you take will solve multiple problems. As you navigate this book, use the worksheet on the following pages to help you better understand the interplay between your challenges and your possible actions. Taking a systems view will help ensure you pick the best actions.

Worksheet Instructions

1. List the symptoms you are experiencing in the left column on the opposite page.

2. For each symptom, list the likely causes. Feel free to eliminate any of the causes we listed; just list the ones you think are cogent in your situation.

3. For each cause, list the actions that you are considering.

4. Now that the chart is complete, look for relationships.

   • Are some of your possible causes leading to multiple symptoms? If so, draw lines connecting them.

   • Are some symptoms causing other symptoms? If yes, then draw lines between them as well.

   • Are certain actions listed more than once? If so circle them.

   • Finally, ask yourself, where is the leverage? What one action (or combination of actions) will solve most of my challenges? Then pursue that path.

Symptoms

Causes

Actions

Notes

Bibliography

Albrecht, Karl. *Service Within: Solving the Middle Management Leadership Crisis*. Homewood, IL: Dow Jones-Irwin, 1990.

Anderson, Howard. "Innovators in Outsourcing." *Forbes*, October 23, 1995.

Appelbaum, Steven. "Revisiting Career Plateauing: Same Old Problems, Avant Garde Solutions," *Journal of Managerial Psychology*, 66, no. 5 (September 1994), p. 12.

Argyris, Chris. "Teaching Smart People How to Learn." *Harvard Business Review*, May/June 1991, pp. 99–109.

Belasco, James and Ralph Stayer. *Flight of the Buffalo*, New York: Warner Books, 1993.

Bennis, Warren G. and Robert Townsend. *Reinventing Leadership: Strategies to Empower the Organization*. New York: Morrow, 1995.

Blaha, Robert. "Forget Functions, Manage Processes." *HR Magazine*, 38 no. 6, June 1993 p. 109.

Blake, Robert and Jane Mouton. *Solving Costly Organizational Conflicts*. San Francisco: Jossey Bass, 1990.

Bluestein, Abram. "A Four-Step Process for Creating Alliances." *Directors and Boards*, Winter 1994.

Bolles, Richard. *What Color Is Your Parachute: A Practical Manual for Job-Hunters*. Berkeley, CA: Ten Speed Press. 1991.

Bowsher, Jack E. *Educating America*. John Wiley, 1989.

Brassard, Michael. *The Memory Jogger Plus*. Methuen, MA: Goal/QPC, 1989.

Bridges, William. *Job Shift: How to Prosper in a Workplace Without Jobs*. Reading, MA: Addison Wesley, 1994.

Bridges, William. "The End of the Job." *Fortune*, September 19, 1994, pp. 62–74.

Bridges, William. *Managing Transitions: Making the Most From Change*. Reading, MA: Addison Wesley, 1991.

Bridges, William. *Surviving Corporate Transition: Rational Management in a World of Mergers, Start-Ups, Takeovers, Layoffs, Divestitures, Deregulation, and New Technologies*. Mill Valley, CA: William Bridges and Associates, 1988.

Brown, Mark Graham. *Baldrige Award Winning Quality*, 6th ed. New York: Quality Resources/ASQC Quality Press, 1996.

Brown, Mark Graham. *Keeping Score: Using the Right Metrics to Drive World-Class Performance*. New York: Quality Resources/AMACOM, 1996.

Brown, Mark Graham; Darcy Hitchcock; and Marsha Willard. *Why TQM Fails and What to Do about It*. Chicago: Irwin Professional Publishing, 1994.

Bureau of National Affairs. "Changing Pay Practices: New Developments in Employee Compensation." Washington, DC: *BNA Labor Relations Week*, 2, no. 24 (June 15, 1988),

Cabana, Steven. "Participative Design Works, Partially Participative Doesn't." *Journal for Quality and Participation*, January/February 1995, pp. 10–19.

Camp, Robert. *Benchmarking: The Search for Industry Best Practices that Lead to Superior Performance*. White Plains, NY: Quality Resources, 1989.

Chang, Richard. *Improving through Benchmarking: A Practical Guide to Achieving Peak Process Performance*. Irvine, CA: Richard Chang Associates, 1994.

Cleveland, William. *The Elements of Graphing Data*. New York: Hobart Press, 1994.

Daniels, Aubrey. *Bringing out the Best in People*. McGraw-Hill, 1994.

Davidow, William and Michael Malone. *The Virtual Corporation: Structuring and Revitalizing the Corporation for the 21st Century*. New York: HarperBusiness, 1992.

Doyle, Robert. *Gain Management*. New York: American Management Association, 1992.

Filipczak, Bob. "Different Strokes: Learning Styles in the Classroom." *TRAINING,* March 1995, pp. 43–48.

Fisher, Roger and William Ury. *Getting to Yes: Negotiating Agreement without Giving in*. Boston: Houghton Mifflin, 1981.

Futrell, David. Ten Reasons Why Surveys Fail: Common Sampling and Measurement Errors. *Quality Progress*, April 1994, pp. 65–69.

Gale, Bradley and Robert Chapman Wood. *Managing Customer Value: Creating Quality and Services that Customers Can See*. New York: Free Press, 1994.

Gardenswartz, Lee and Anita Rowe. *The Managing Diversity Survival Guide: A Complete Collection of Checklists, Activities, and Tips*. Homewood, IL: Irwin Professional Publishing, 1994.

Gendelman, Joel. "Talking Ain't Teaching." *Performance and Instruction* 30, no. 4 (April 1991), p. 4.

Gendelman, Joel. "Talking Ain't Teaching—Part 1." *Performance and Instruction*, 30 no. 5 (May/June 1991), p. 24.

Gendelman, Joel. "Talking Ain't Teaching—Part 2." *Performance and Instruction*, 30 no. 6 (July 1991), p. 21.

Gendelman, Joel. "Talking Ain't Teaching—Part 3." *Performance and Instruction*, 30 no. 7 (August 1991), p. 26.

Gendelman, Joel. "Talking Ain't Teaching—Part 4." *Performance and Instruction*, 30 no. 8 (September 199), p. 1.

Gendelman, Joel. "Talking Ain't Teaching—Part 5." *Performance and Instruction*, 30 no. 9 (October 1991), p. 26.

Gerson, Richard. *Measuring Customer Satisfaction*. Menlo Park, CA: Crisp Publications, 1993.

Ghoshal, Sumantra and Christopher Bartlett. "Changing the Role of Top Management: Beyond Structure to Processes." *Harvard Business Review,* January/February 1995, pp. 86–96.

Gordon, Jack. "Different from What? Diversity as a Performance Issue." *TRAINING*, May 1995, pp. 25–34.

Hamel, Gary and C. K. Prahalad. *Competing for the Future*. Boston, MA: Harvard Business Press, 1994.

Hammer, Michael. "Reengineering Work: Don't Automate, Obliterate!" *Harvard Business Review*, July/August 1990, pp. 104–112.

Hammer, Michael and James Champy. *Reengineering Work: A Manifesto for Business Revolution*. New York: Harper Business, 1993.

Harrington, H. James. *Business Process Improvement: The Breakthrough Strategy for Total Quality, Productivity, and Competitiveness* NY: McGraw Hill, 1991.

Hauser, John and Don Clausing. "The House of Quality." *Harvard Business Review*, May/June 1988, pp. 63–73.

Hayes, Bob E. *Measuring Customer Satisfaction: Development and Use of Questionnaires*. Milwaukee, WI: Quality Press, 1992.

Henderson, Rebecca. "Managing Innovation in the Information Age." *Harvard Business Review,* January/February 1994, pp. 100–105.

Hequet, Marc. "Flat and Happy." *TRAINING*, April 1995, pp. 29–34.

Herzberg, Frederick. "One More Time: How Do You Motivate Employees?" *Harvard Business Review*, January/February 1968,

Hitchcock, Darcy. *The Work Redesign Team Handbook: A Step-by-Step Guide to Creating Self-Directed Teams*. White Plains, NY: Quality Resources, 1994.

Hitchcock, Darcy. "What Will We Find in an Intrapreneur's Rabbit Hole?" *Journal for Quality and Participation*, December 1993.

Hitchcock, Darcy. "The Engine of Empowerment." *Journal for Quality and Participation*, March 1992, p. 50.

Hitchcock, Darcy. "Building Instructional Games." *TRAINING*, March 1988.

Hitchcock, Darcy and Marsha Willard. *Why Teams Can Fail and What to Do About It*. Homewood, IL: Irwin Professional Publishing, 1995.

Hitchcock, Darcy; Marsha Willard; and Ed Warnock. *The Catalytic Leadership Handbook*. Portland, OR: Portland State University, 1993.

Holland, John. *Making Vocational Choices: A Theory of Vocational Personalities and Work Environments*. Englewood Cliffs, NJ: Prentice Hall, 1985.

Howard, Philip K. *The Death of Common Sense: How Law Is Suffocating America*. New York: Random House, 1994.

Hronec, Steven. *Vital Signs*. New York: AMACOM, 1993.

Isaacs, William. "Taking Flight: Dialogue, Collective Thinking, and Organizational Learning." *Organizational Dynamics*, Fall 1993, pp. 24–39.

Jacobs, Robert. *Real-Time Strategic Change: How to Involve an Entire Organization in Fast and Far-Reaching Change*. San Francisco: Berrett Koehler, 1994.

Jamieson, David and O'Mara, Julie. *Managing Workforce 2000*. San Francisco: Jossey Bass Publishers, 1991.

Jones, Louis and Ronald McBride. *An Introduction to Team Approach Problem Solving*. Milwaukee, WI: Quality Press, 1992.

Kanter, Rosabeth Moss. *When Giants Learn to Dance: Mastering the Challenge of Strategy, Management, and Careers in the 1990's*. New York: Simon & Schuster, 1989.

Kaplan, Robert and David Norton. "Putting the Balanced Scorecard to Work." *Harvard Business Review*, September/October 1993, p. 134.

Kaplan, Robert and David Norton. "The Balanced Scorecard—Measures that Drive Performance." *Harvard Business Review*, January/February 1992, p. 71.

Katzenbach, Jon and Douglas Smith. *The Wisdom of Teams*. New York: Harper Business, 1993.

Kelly, Robert and Janet Caplan. "How Bell Labs Creates Star Performers." *Harvard Business Review*, July/August 1993, pp. 128–139.

Kilmann, Ralph. *Beyond the Quick Fix: Managing Five Tracks to Organizational Success*. San Francisco: Jossey-Bass, 1984.

Kilmann, Ralph and Ines. *Making Organizations Competitive: Enhancing Networks and Relationships across Traditional Boundaries*. San Francisco: Jossey Bass, 1991.

Kim, Daniel. "The Link between Individual and Organizational Learning." *Sloan Management Review*, Fall 1993, pp. 37–50.

Klubnik, Joan. *Rewarding and Recognizing Employees: Ideas for Individuals, Teams, and Managers*. Chicago: Irwin Professional Publishers, 1995.

Knouse, Stephen. *The Reward and Recognition Process in Total Quality Management*. Milwaukee, WI: Quality Press, 1995.

Kofman, Fred and Peter Senge. "Communities of Commitment: The Heart of Learning Organizations." *Organizational Dynamics*, Fall 1993, pp. 5–23.

Kohn, Alfie. *Punished by Rewards: The Trouble with Gold Stars, Incentive Plans, A's, Praise and Other Bribes*. New York: Houghton Mifflin Company, 1993.

Kolodny, Harvey and Barbara Dresner. "Linking Arrangements and New Work Designs." *Organization Dynamics* 14, no. 3 (Winter 1986), pp. 33–51.

Kotter, John. *The New Rules: How to Succeed in Today's Post Corporate World*. New York: Free Press, 1995.

Lawler, Edward. *Strategic Pay: Aligning Organizational Strategies and Pay Systems*. San Francisco: Jossey Bass, 1990.

Lewis, Jordan. *Partnerships for Profit: Structuring and Managing Strategic Alliances*. Free Press, 1990.

Main, Jeremy. "Betting on the 21st Century Jet" *Fortune*, April 20, 1992, p. 102.

McCall, Morgan; Michael Lombardo; and Ann Morrison. *The Lessons of Experience: How Successful Executives Develop on the Job*. Lexington, MA: Lexington Books, 1988.

Montgomery, Douglas. *Design and Analysis of Experiments*. Milwaukee, WI: Quality Press, 1991.

Moody, Patricia. *Break-Through Partnering: Creating a Collective Enterprise Advantage*. Essex Junction, VT: Oliver Wight Publications, 1993.

Myers, Isabel and Peter. *Gifts Differing*. Palo Alto, CA: Consulting Psychologists Press, 1980.

Nadler, Gerald and Shozo Hibino. *Breakthrough Thinking: Why We Must Change the Way We Solve Problems, and the Seven Principles to Achieve This*. Rocklin, CA: Prima Publishing and Communications, 1990.

Nelson, Bob. *1001 Ways to Reward Employees*. New York: Workman Publishers, 1993.

Noer, David. *Healing the Wounds*. San Francisco: Jossey Bass, 1993.

Oregon Progress Board. *Oregon Benchmarks: Standards for Measuring Statewide Progress and Institutional Performance*. Salem, OR: Oregon Progress Board, 1994.

Osborne, David and Ted Gaebler. *Reinventing Government*. Reading, MA: Addison Wesley, 1992.

Pasmore, William. *Designing Effective Organizations: The Sociotechnical Systems Perspective*. New York: John Wiley & Sons, 1988.

Peters, Tom. *Liberation Management: Necessary Disorganization for the Nanosecond Nineties*. New York: Alfred A. Knopf, 1992.

Pinchot, Gifford and Elizabeth Pinchot. *The End of Bureaucracy and the Rise of the Intelligent Organization*. San Francisco: Berrett Koehler, 1993.

Pinchot, Gifford, III. *Intrapreneuring: Why You Don't Have to Leave the Corporation to Become an Entrepreneur*. New York: Harper and Row, 1985.

Port, Otis. "Quality: Small and Midsize Companies Seize the Challenge—Not a Moment too Soon." *Business Week*, November 30, 1992, p. 66.

Prahalad, C. K. and Gary Hamel. "The Core Competence of the Corporation." *Harvard Business Review*, May/June 1990, pp. 79–91.

Rackham, Neil. *SPIN Selling*. New York: McGraw Hill, 1988.

Rackham, Neil. *Major Account Sales Strategy*. New York: McGraw Hill, 1989.

Ricardo, Semler. *Maverick: The Success Story Behind the World's Most Unusual Workplace*. New York: Warner Books, 1993.

Rifkin, Glenn. "A Skeptic's Guide to Groupware." *Forbes* ASAP Supplement, June 5, 1995, pp. 76–81.

Rigby, Darrell and Robin Buchanan. "Putting More Strategy into Strategic Alliances." *Directors and Boards*, Winter 1994.

Robbins, Anthony. *Unlimited Power: The New Science of Personal Achievement*. New York: Simon & Schuster, 1986.

Ross, Rick. "Skillful Discussions," in Peter Senge. *The Fifth Discipline Fieldbook*. New York: Doubleday, 1994, p. 391.

Rummler, Geary and Alan Brache. *Improving Performance: How to Manage the White Space on the Organization Chart*. San Francisco: Jossey Bass, 1990.

Ryan, Alan. *Statistical Methods for Quality Improvement*. New York: Wiley, 1989.

Ryan, Kathleen and Daniel Oestreich. *Driving Fear out of the Workplace: How to Overcome the Invisible Barriers to Quality, Productivity, and Innovations*. San Francisco: Jossey Bass, 1991.

Schein, Edgar. *Organizational Culture and Leadership*. San Francisco: Jossey Bass, 1995.

Schein, Edgar. "On Dialogue, Culture, and Organizational Learning." *Organizational Dynamics*, Fall 1993, pp. 40–51.

Scholtes. Peter. *The Team Handbook: How to Use Teams to Improve Quality*. Madison, WI: Joiner & Associates, 1990.

Senge, Peter. *Fifth Discipline Fieldbook*. New York: Currency Doubleday, 1994.

Senge, Peter. *The Fifth Discipline: The Art and Practice of the Learning Organization*. New York: Doubleday, 1990.

Sher, Barbara and Annie Gottlieb. *Wishcraft: How to Get What You Really Want*. New York: Ballantine Books, 1983.

Spendolini, Michael. *The Benchmarking Book*. New York: AMACOM, 1992.

Stack, Jack. *The Great Game of Business*. New York: Doubleday, 1994.

Stamps, David. "Cyberinterviews Combat Turnover." *TRAINING*, April 1995, pp. 43–47.

Stayer, Ralph. "How I Learned to Let My Employees Lead." *Harvard Business Review*, November/December 1990, p. 66.

Svenson, Raynold A. and Monica J. Rinderer. *The Training and Development Strategic Plan Workbook*. New Jersey: Prentice Hall, 1992.

Tague, Nancy. *The Quality Toolbox*. Milwaukee, WI: Quality Press, 1995.

Treacy, Michael and Fred Wiersema. *The Discipline of Market Leaders: Choose Your Customers, Narrow Your Focus, Dominate Your Markets*. Reading, MA: Addison Wesley, 1995.

Tuckman, B. W. "Developmental Sequence in Small Groups." *Psychological Bulletin*, 63, no. 6, pp. 384–399.

Ulrich, Dave, Todd Jick, and Mary Ann Von Glinow. "High-Impact Learning: Building and Diffusing Learning Capability." *Organizational Dynamics*, Fall 1993, pp. 52–66.

Ury, William. *Getting Past No: Negotiating with Difficult People*. New York: Bantam Books, 1991.

Wack, Pierre. "Scenarios: Shooting the Rapids." *Harvard Business Review*, November/December 1985, p. 139.

Wack, Pierre. "Scenarios: Uncharted Waters Ahead." *Harvard Business Review*, September/October 1985, p. 72.

Watson, Gregory. *Strategic Benchmarking: How to Rate Your Company's Performance against the World's Best*. New York: J. Wiley and Sons, 1993.

Weisbord, Marvin. *Discovering Common Ground: How Future Search Conferences Bring People Together to Achieve Breakthrough Innovation, Empowerment, Shared Vision, and Collaborative Action*. San Francisco: Berrett-Koehler Publishers, 1993.

Weisbord, Marvin. *Productive Workplaces: Organizing and Managing for Dignity, Meaning and Community*. San Francisco: Jossey Bass, 1987.

Weisbord, Marvin and Sandra Janoff. *Future Search*. San Francisco: Berrett-Koehler, 1995.

Wheatley, Margaret J. *Leadership and the New Science*. San Francisco: Berrett-Koehler Publishers, 1992.

Whiteley, Richard. *The Customer-Driven Company: Moving from Talk to Action*. Reading, MA: Addison-Wesley, 1991.

Wilson, Thomas. *Innovative Reward Systems for the Changing Workplace*. Milwaukee, WI: Quality Press, 1995.

Zemke, Ron and Tom Kramlinger. *Figuring Things Out*. Reading, MA: Addison Wesley, 1984.

Zuckerman, Marilyn and Lewis Hatala. *Incredibly American*. ASQC Quality Press, 1992.

The Malcolm Baldrige National Quality Award criteria may be obtained free of charge from

Malcolm Baldrige National Quality Award

National Institute of Standards and Technology

Route 270 and Quince Orchard Road

Administration Building, Room A537

Gaithersburg, MD 20899-0001

Telephone: 301-975-2036 FAX: 301-948-3716

Index

For ease of identification, all entries that are "symptoms" are set in **bold-face type.**